Look, Learn & Create

Origami

QUARRY

Brimming with creative inspiration, how-to projects, and useful information to enrich your everyday life, Quarto Knows is a favorite destination for those pursuing their interests and passions. Visit our site and dig deeper with our books into your area of interest: Quarto Creates, Quarto Cooks, Quarto Homes, Quarto Lives, Quarto Drives, Quarto Explores, Quarto Gifts, or Quarto Kids.

© 2011 Quarto Publishing Group USA Inc.

This paperback edition published in 2018

First Published in 2011 by Creative Publishing international, an imprint of
The Quarto Group, 100 Cummings Center, Suite 265-D, Beverly, MA 01915, USA.
T (978) 282-9590 F (978) 283-2742
QuartoKnows.com

Quarry Books titles are also available at discount for retail, wholesale, promotional, and bulk purchase. For details, contact the Special Sales Manager by email at specialsales@quarto.com or by mail at The Quarto Group, Attn: Special Sales Manager, 401 Second Avenue North, Suite 310, Minneapolis, MN 55401, USA.

10 9 8 7 6 5 4 3 2 1

ISBN: 978-1-63159-655-1

Digital edition published in 2018
eISBN: 978-1-61060-194-8

Originally found under the following Library of Congress Cataloging-in-Publication Data
Coleman, Benjamin John.
Origami 101 / Benjamin Coleman.
p. cm.
Summary: "Beginner's guide to origami, with instructions, photos, and diagrams for folding fifty paper figures." Provided by publisher.
ISBN-13: 978-1-58923-606-6 (hard cover)
ISBN-10: 1-58923-606-8 (hard cover)
1. Origami. I. Title.
TT870.C6163 2011
736'.982--dc22
     2010046926

Photography, Illustrations, and Videography:
Benjamin John Coleman
Cover & Book Design: Mighty Media
Page Layout: Danielle Smith

Printed in China

CONTENTS

Introduction

Origami literally means "fold paper" in Japanese. Ori means fold and gami, or kami in Japanese, means paper. The art form was started in China and then brought to Japan where it became quite popular by 1614.

Traditional origami is performed on a square that is colored on one side. There is no tearing or cutting allowed.

Origami folding patterns have been used in the design of spacecraft parts since the 1980s when Koryo Miura's origami-based solar panels flew on a Japanese rocket.

A mass-produced origami folding pattern is as close to you as the air bag in your car. The first mass-produced origami flower was introduced in 2010 by the author of this book.

Origami is increasingly used in engineering consumer products. Cellular phones with self-folding antennae for better reception and microchips that automatically reconfigure themselves through folding are likely under development.

One newer origami technique is called "crumple folding," where the paper is crumpled rather than folded. This has led to highly complex paper models that cannot be repeated exactly.

Origami has moved beyond traditional squares. The flowers on this page were made with a star shape, which is then folded using an origami pattern, but a glass cutter is used to impress the folds on the paper first.

How to Use This Book

This book was designed by an origami enthusiast to teach those unfamiliar with origami how to fold. Directions for folding origami figures always include symbols, and the key to success is learning what these symbols mean and how to execute them. Rather than create a long introductory chapter consisting of folding symbols and their descriptions, folding symbols are explained as they are encountered. Each folding symbol is explained in a blue box near the step where it is introduced in a pattern. This gives you immediate explanation of a new symbol. Detailed photographs help you along the way. You will find a Symbol Index Bookmark at the back of the book, which shows the folding symbols and the page numbers where they are explained. You can cut out one bookmark to mark pages while you

fold and keep the other one in the book for quick reference. Whenever you don't remember what a symbol means, just flip to the Symbol Index and turn to the page indicated.

The DVD-ROM included with this book is an additional learning tool that will show you how to fold each of the models presented in the book. The models are arranged in chapters just like the book contents. Whenever you are having difficulty folding a model, select that model from the DVD menu and watch the steps. The disk also contains files for printing additional origami paper from your home computer and printer. It is both PC and Mac compatible, and can be viewed using Quicktime software. To download the latest version of Quicktime for free, visit http:/www.apple.com/quicktime/download.

blue boxes explain symbols

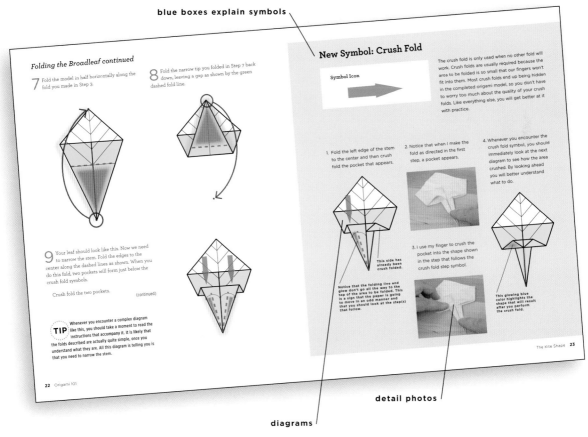

diagrams

detail photos

New Symbol: Glow and Afterglow

Symbol Icon

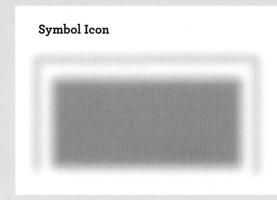

Learning a three-dimensional art form like origami from a two-dimensional page isn't easy. One of the advances you will find in the diagrams in this book and on the accompanying DVD is called glowfold. Glowfold tells you what surface is going to move during a fold and where it went after it was folded.

A surface that is about to be folded will glow with a red hue on top of it. In the diagram that follows, you will see afterglow. This afterglow not only tells you what surface moved, but it also tells you where the open edges should be and how to confirm the orientation of your paper. The afterglow will only be present in the step immediately following a step where glow was present. Here is an example of how it works:

1. A square is being folded in half horizontally. The surface that will move glows.

2. After folding, glow escapes from the open edges. Notice that glow does not escape from the folded edge.

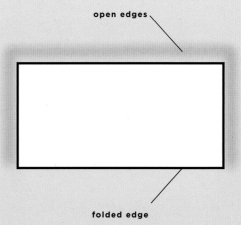

open edges

folded edge

New Symbol: Fold

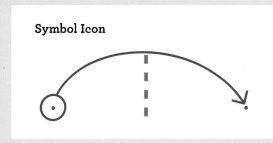

Symbol Icon

The fold symbol consists of a purple arc with an arrowhead on one end and a circle on the other. A green dashed (or occasionally a red dotted and dashed) line will appear underneath and perpendicular to it. This is probably the most common, powerful, and easy-to-master symbol in origami.

It is important that you learn the proper way to make a fold. The quality of your finished origami model is directly related to your ability to align the paper and then impress the fold into it. Every fold you make should conform to the following steps:

1. Figure out what the diagram is telling you. This diagram tells us to fold the paper in half horizontally, bottom to top.

2. Reorient your square so making the fold is as comfortable and easy as possible. In this case, to precisely align the edges, I rotate the square 90 degrees before folding it.

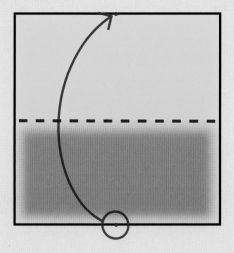

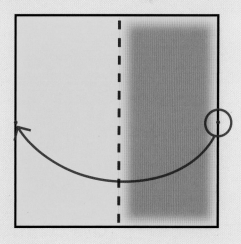

(continued)

New Symbol: Fold continued

3. Lift the area to be folded off the work surface.

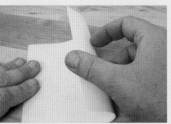

4. Align the edge, curling the area to be folded. Hold the aligned edge in place for the remainder of these steps.

5. Gently push down the area along what will become the fold line.

6. Carefully align the edge. Once aligned, use one hand to hold the edge securely while you...

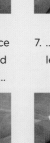

7. ...slide your finger down the length of the fold.

8. To sharpen the fold, slide your fingernail along the length of it.

This is what this sequence will look like in folding diagrams in this book:

1. Fold the square in half horizontally.

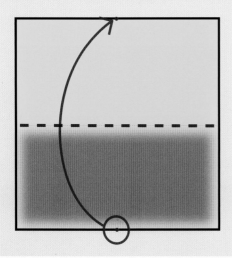

2. Your model should look like this. Notice the afterglow around the left, right, and top edges. These are open edges, as opposed to the bottom edge, which is closed by the fold I just made.

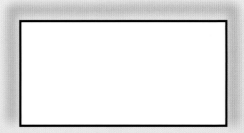

New Symbol: Flip

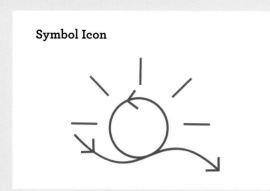

Symbol Icon

The difficulty expressed by the graph (pictured at left) is a little bit misleading. While flipping your paper is among the easiest things you will ever do, the flip symbol is the most commonly overlooked symbol in origami. If your model suddenly bears little resemblance to what you see in a diagram, go back and review the last few steps. You may have missed the flip symbol. Make a mental note to notice these symbols!

1. Flip your paper.

2. Your paper should look like this.

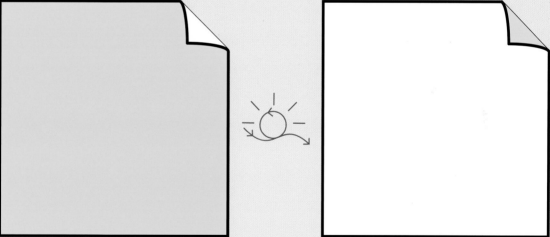

Making Practice Paper

It is easy to make practice paper once you know how to do it. You should always use practice paper when attempting a new model. Practice paper is inexpensive, so if you make a mistake it won't bother you too much. I use regular 8½ × 11 inch (European size A4) printer paper.

1 Fold a piece of printer paper in half.

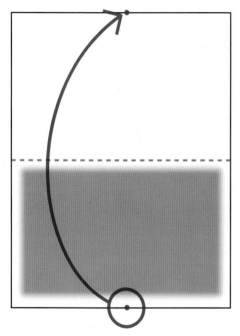

2 Fold the upper left-hand corner of the top layer of paper diagonally down to the fold you made in Step 1.

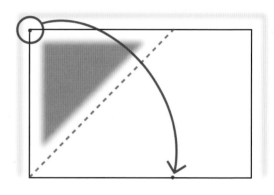

3 Your paper should look like this. Now flip it left to right.

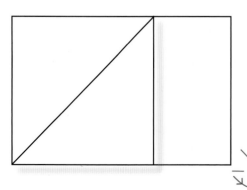

4 Fold the remaining upper right-hand corner diagonally to the fold you made in Step 1.

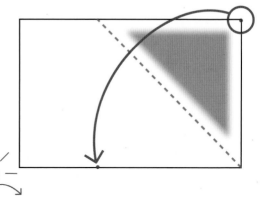

5 Your paper should look like this.

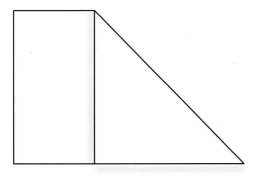

6 Cut along the edge of the triangle (do not cut the triangle itself) as shown by the dashed line. The area you cut off will not be used and can be put in your recycle bin. Completely unfold the triangle.

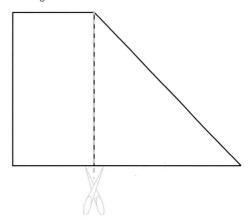

7 Cut your paper in half and you will have two practice squares. Each practice square will have a diagonal crease.

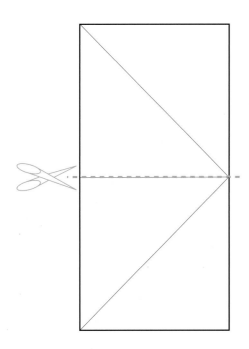

8 You can color one side of your paper yellow to make it match the diagrams and photographs in this book. Make sure you put a piece of newspaper under your square to protect your work surface.

TIP Always work on a smooth, flat surface. You can use a plastic putty knife or wooden ruler to sharpen folds. Do not use any tool with metal edges, as you will damage both your paper and your work surface.

The Kite Shape

We begin with one of the simplest origami shapes. While the initial shape might seem simple, it has great potential. This chapter is composed of projects ordered in a logical progression, from simple to complex. Each project builds on the previous one, so projects should be completed in the order they are presented.

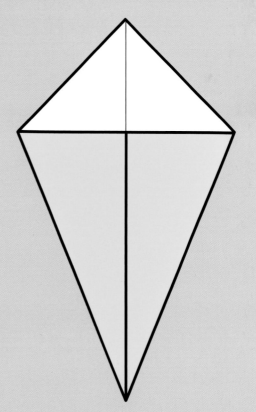

Folding the Kite Shape

1 Begin with the colored side of your paper facing down.

2 Fold the square in half diagonally.

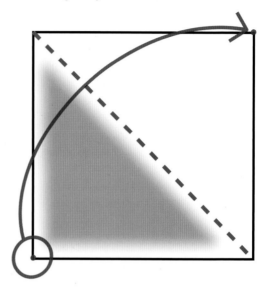

3 Unfold the fold you made in Step 2.

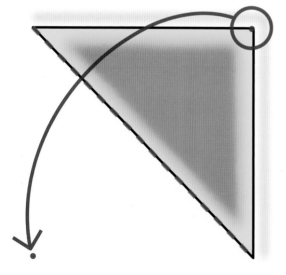

4 Fold the bottom left corner to the fold you made in Step 2.

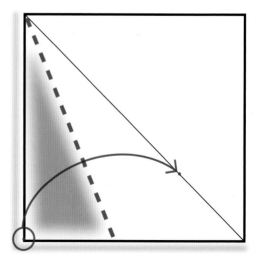

5 Your paper should look like this.

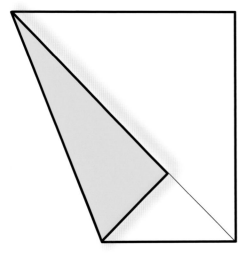

6 Fold the top right corner to the fold you made in Step 2.

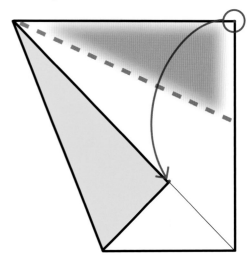

7 Your paper should look like this.

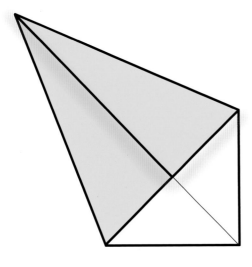

8 Reorient your paper as shown. This is called the "kite shape." It is a powerful origami shape from which many models can be folded. In future folding diagrams this shape will appear as the first step, which means you should return to this section to fold it.

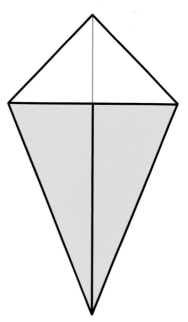

Folding the Penguin

1 Begin with the kite shape (page 14). If you're using swan paper, start with the beak color at the bottom.

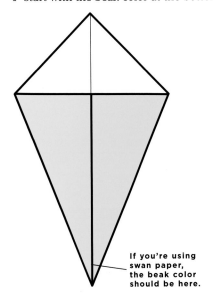

If you're using swan paper, the beak color should be here.

2 Fold the corner of the top layer of paper down and to the left as shown.

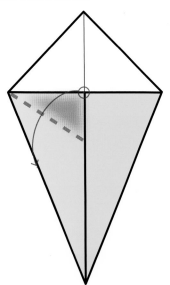

3 Fold the other corner in the same manner.

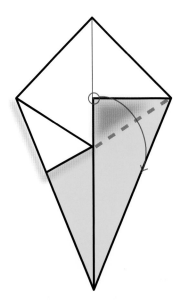

4 Your model should look like this. Flip it.

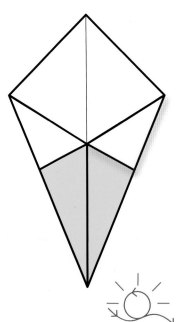

5 Fold the top corner down. Notice that the fold line extends from the left corner to the right corner.

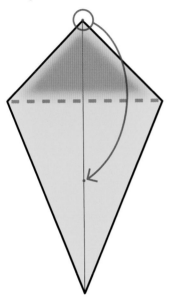

6 Fold the model in half vertically.

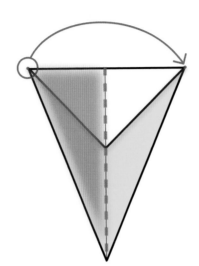

7 Fold the bottom tip up and to the left as shown.

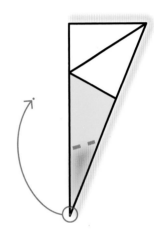

8 Your model should look like this.

9 Reorient your model so the head is on the top and you'll have a penguin!

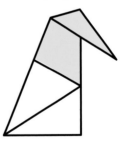

Other Things You Can Do

Revisit the penguin after you have folded a loon. You can obtain a better looking penguin by performing an outside reverse fold on the head.

The penguin uses both sides of your paper. Try creating a two-colored penguin by coloring both sides of the paper in different colors.

Folding the Broad Leaf

1 Begin with the kite shape (page 14) and flip it.

2 Fold the kite shape in half vertically along the fold that is already there.

3 Fold and then unfold your leaf in half horizontally as shown.

(continued)

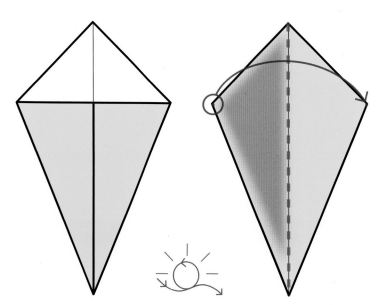

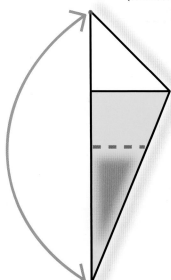

New Symbol: Fold and Then Unfold

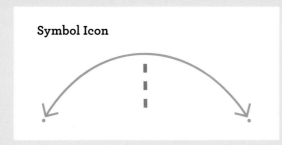

Symbol Icon

The fold and then unfold symbol is a blue arc with arrowheads on both ends. A green dashed (or occasionally red dotted and dashed) line will accompany it. It is commonly mistaken for the fold symbol but the mistake is usually quickly detected. The fold and then unfold symbol means just that, fold as if it were the fold symbol, and then unfold.

The fold and then unfold symbol is basically an abbreviation, allowing us to leave out a diagram but still accurately convey what is being folded and unfolded. Here is a series of diagrams that illustrates this point:

1. Fold the paper in half horizontally.

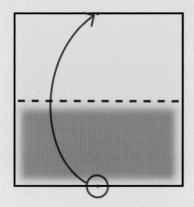

2. Unfold the fold you made in Step 1.

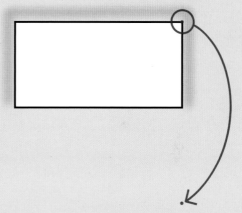

3. Your paper should look like this.

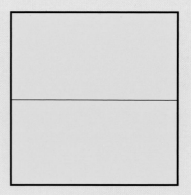

(continued)

New Symbol: Fold and Then Unfold continued

Here's what the fold and then unfold symbol will look like in a series of diagrams:

1. Fold and then unfold the square in half horizontally.

2. Your paper should look like this. Notice that there is no afterglow after the fold and then unfold symbol.

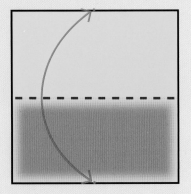
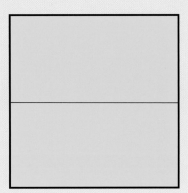

Folding the Broadleaf continued

4 To fold some veins into the leaf, fold and then unfold the top tip down and to the right, using the fold we made in Step 3 as a guide.

5 Fold and then unfold a few more veins into your leaf above and parallel to the vein you folded in Step 3. Do not fold veins below the fold you made in Step 3.

6 Unfold the fold you made in Step 2 and then flip your model.

(continued)

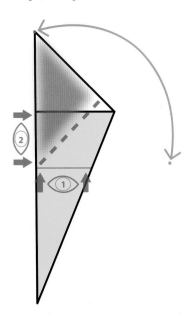
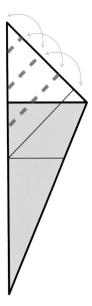
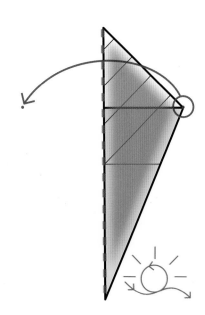

New Symbol: Alignment

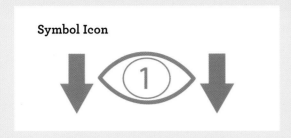

Symbol Icon

The alignment symbol helps you make more accurate folds. This symbol always appears in pairs, telling you to align one edge, or fold, to another edge or fold. By carefully aligning the two edges or folds, you can achieve great accuracy in your work and a better final model.

Each alignment symbol's arrows point to an edge or a previously folded line. Inside the circle there will be a number. The number will then be referred to in that step's folding direction.

1. Fold the bottom left corner up and to the right as shown, aligning (1) with (2).

2. The gap between the edge of the paper (alignment symbol 1) and the pre-existing fold (alignment symbol 2) determines the quality of your alignment. If your paper's edge goes beyond the pre-existing fold, you have an alignment of low quality. If your paper's edge is very close to the pre-existing fold, you have an alignment of high quality.

A crease folded in a previous step.

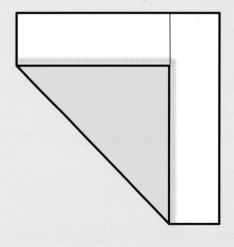

Folding the Broadleaf continued

7 Fold the model in half horizontally along the fold you made in Step 3.

8 Fold the narrow tip you folded in Step 7 back down, leaving a gap as shown by the green dashed fold line.

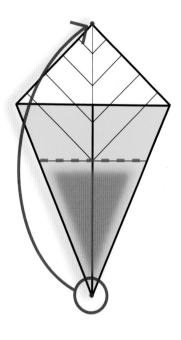

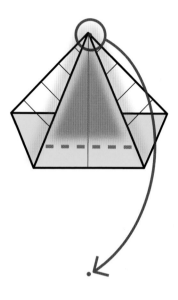

9 Your leaf should look like this. Now we need to narrow the stem. Fold the edges to the center along the dashed lines as shown. When you do this fold, two pockets will form just below the crush fold symbols.

Crush fold the two pockets.

(continued)

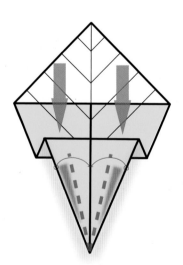

TIP Whenever you encounter a complex diagram like this, you should take a moment to read the instructions that accompany it. It is likely that the folds described are actually quite simple, once you understand what they are. All this diagram is telling you is that you need to narrow the stem.

New Symbol: Crush Fold

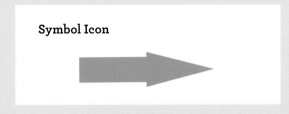

Symbol Icon

The crush fold is only used when no other fold will work. Crush folds are usually required because the area to be folded is so small that our fingers won't fit into them. Most crush folds end up being hidden in the completed origami model, so you don't have to worry too much about the quality of your crush folds. Like everything else, you will get better at it with practice.

1. Fold the left edge of the stem to the center and then crush fold the pocket that appears.

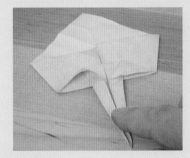

This side has already been crush folded.

Notice that the folding line and glow don't go all the way to the top of the area to be folded. This is a sign that the paper is going to move in an odd manner and that you should look at the step(s) that follow.

2. Notice that when I make the fold as directed in the first step, a pocket appears.

3. I use my finger to crush the pocket into the shape shown in the step that follows the crush fold step symbol.

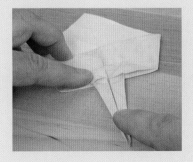

4. Whenever you encounter the crush fold symbol, you should immediately look at the next diagram to see how the area crushed. By looking ahead you will better understand what to do.

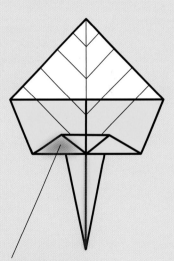

This glowing blue color highlights the shape that will result after you perform the crush fold.

Folding the Broadleaf continued

10 Your model should look like this. Narrow the stem by pinch folding it.

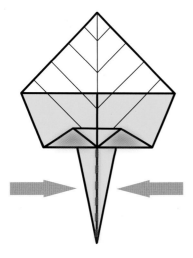

If you flip your leaf, it should look like this. Now we'll shape it so it looks more like a real leaf.

11 Place your index and middle fingers of your left hand under the stem connection of the leaf. Put your thumb on top. Pinch the stem with your right hand while you push your thumb down and fingers up with your left hand. This will force the surface of the leaf up.

12 Push down with your thumbs at the base of the leaf to complete shaping.

New Symbol: Pinch Fold

Symbol Icon

The pinch fold symbol tells you to pinch an area between your thumb and index finger. Usually it is used to narrow an area. In this example we use the pinch fold to narrow the stem of a leaf.

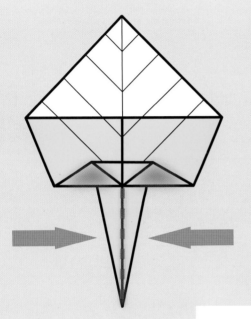

1. The pinch fold symbols direct us to narrow the stem of this leaf.

2. Lift your model off your work surface to complete a pinch fold.

Other Things You Can Do

Origami leaves can be a lot of fun. The smaller you make them, the more delicate and lifelike they will look. You can glue your leaves onto branches and make beautiful works of art. I call this art form "Origami Bonsai" and have written three books on the subject.

You can color your leaves with crayons or markers, or you can use the paper supplied with this book. I made the origami bonsai pictured here from a branch I found. It has eight leaves, which I made by cutting two of the squares (into quarters) that came with this book.

New Symbol: Mountain and Valley Folds—Basic

Symbol Icon

We use a red dotted and dashed line to represent a mountain fold in diagrams; a green dashed line to represent a valley fold. The vast majority of the folds in this book are valley folds. For now, all you need to know is the difference.

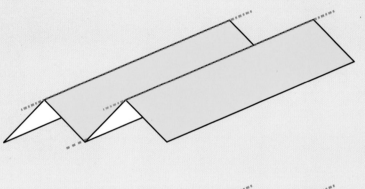

The paper on either side of a mountain fold slopes down, and on either side of a valley fold it slopes up.

Remember: Green valleys and red mountaintops.

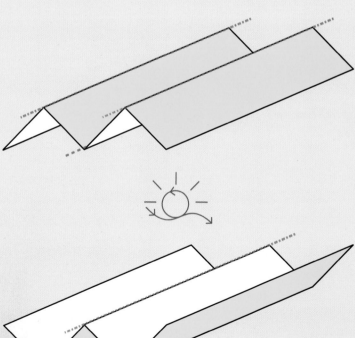

Here's the confusing part. If you flip the same piece of paper, the folds reverse.

For our purpose right now, all mountain and valley folds simply describe how the paper looks now and how we want it to look in the next step.

Folding the Loon

1 Begin by flipping the kite shape (page 14). If you're using swan paper, the beak color should be at the bottom.

2 Fold in half vertically along the fold line that is already there.

(continued)

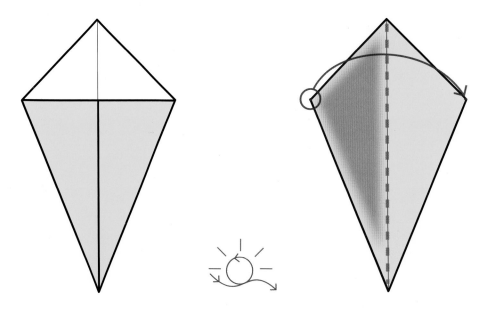

New Symbol: Outside Reverse Fold

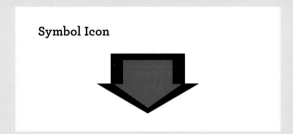

Symbol Icon

The outside reverse fold is key to many origami models. At first it will seem challenging, but with only a little practice this maneuver will become second nature to you. The key to easily performing an outside reverse fold is to make sure you have sharpened the fold to be manipulated. The symbol for this fold is a red arrow with black on the outside.

1. Sharpen the fold the arrow is pointing at.

2. Unfold the fold you made in the step that preceded the reverse fold symbol.

3. An outside reverse fold always involves the layer of paper that lies beneath it. In Step 4 of the loon we will fold two layers of the kite shape. This means we will need to open the model back to the kite shape.

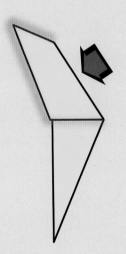

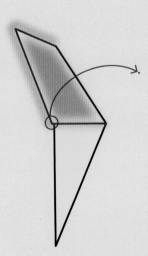

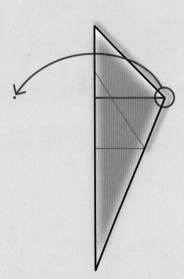

(continued)

New Symbol: Outside Reverse Fold *continued*

Remember: Green valleys and red mountaintops.

This is what your paper will look like if you unfold it after completing the outside reverse fold.

4. Lift the paper off the work surface. Put your middle fingers under the longer fold that needs to be reversed. Use your index fingers and thumbs to bend the paper over your middle fingers. The paper should bend only along the fold, provided that you sharpened it sufficiently.

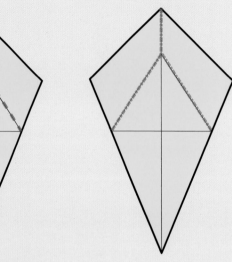

This is what your paper looks like now. It has two valley folds and one mountain fold. An outside reverse fold means that all three of these folds will become mountain folds.

5. The fold will begin to become a mountain fold. Once this happens, remove your middle fingers and pinch the fold closed.

6. The second, smaller fold just needs to be pinched to complete the outside reverse fold.

Reorient your model. Your model should look like this.

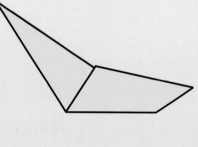

Folding the Loon *continued*

3 Fold in half horizontally by lifting the bottom point to the top and then unfold.

4 Fold the right corner of both layers of paper down and to the left using the fold you made in Step 3 as a guide. After folding, the paper will extend a little bit beyond the left edge. Run your finger over the fold to sharpen it.

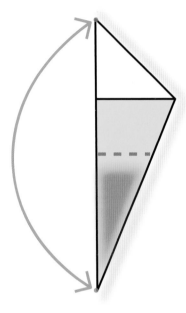

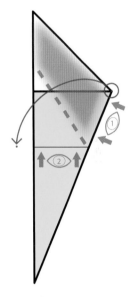

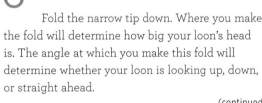

5 Perform an outside reverse fold on the fold you made in Step 4.

6 Reorient your model. It should look like this.

Fold the narrow tip down. Where you make the fold will determine how big your loon's head is. The angle at which you make this fold will determine whether your loon is looking up, down, or straight ahead.

(continued)

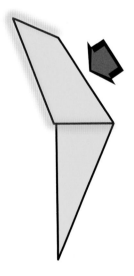

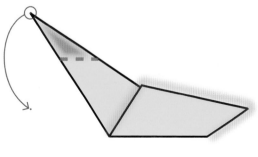

Folding the Loon continued

7 Perform an inside reverse fold on the fold you made in Step 6.

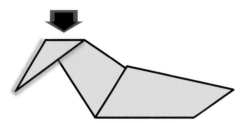

8 Your completed loon should look like this.

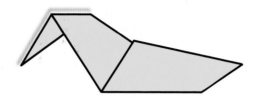

Other Things You Can Do

In Step 6 you can make the loon's head larger or smaller by folding it closer or further from the narrow tip.

If you change the angle of the fold in Step 6, you can make your loon look up or down.

You can change the size of the loon's body by moving the fold you made in Step 4. You will also discover that the fold we made in Step 3 was not required. It was only for alignment.

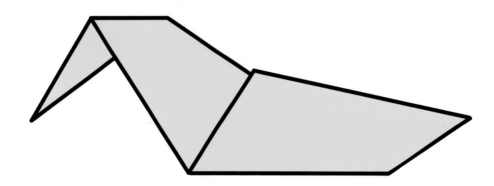

New Symbol: Inside Reverse Fold

Symbol Icon

The inside reverse fold can be used for making many origami appendages, like the legs and heads of animals. The symbol differs from the outside reverse fold in that the black arrow is on the inside rather than the outside.

Don't worry about confusing the inside reverse fold with the outside reverse fold. It is not possible to make an outside reverse fold where an inside reverse fold is required, and the other way around, it is not possible to make an inside reverse fold where an outside reverse fold is required.

1. The inside reverse fold symbol points at the fold that needs to be changed. Make sure you sharpen this fold before proceeding.

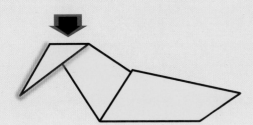

2. Unfold the fold you made in the step that preceded the inside reverse fold symbol.

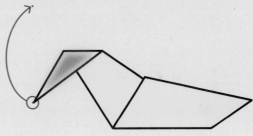

3. Now you need to determine the layers of paper the inside reverse fold affects. The inside reverse fold always affects at least two layers. In this case, we will have to unfold our model back to the kite shape.

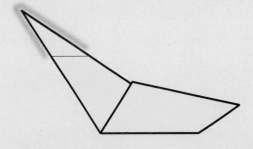

(continued)

New Symbol: Inside Reverse Fold continued

4. This diagram depicts the folds in the area to be modified as they are now.

5. This is the folding pattern we want: two mountain folds with a valley in between. The following pictures should help guide you to completing this fold successfully.

6. Position your middle fingers under the folds you want to make mountain folds and use your index fingers and thumbs to push the paper down.

7. Pinch the folds to secure them.

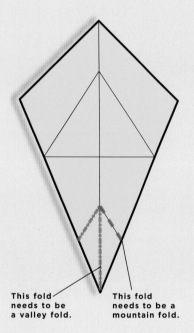

This fold needs to be a valley fold.

This fold needs to be a mountain fold.

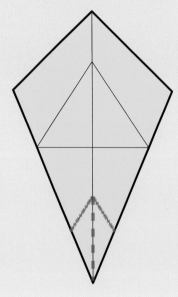

8. Fold the model in half and pinch the folds you've just made to secure them.

When you finish the inside reverse fold, your model should look like this.

Remember: Green valleys and red mountaintops.

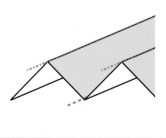

Folding the Roosting Robin

1 Begin with the kite shape (page 14). Fold and then unfold your model in half horizontally and then flip it.

2 Fold and then unfold the bottom tip up and to the left using the fold you made in Step 1 and the bottom right edge as a guide.

3 Fold and then unfold the bottom tip up and to the right using the fold you made in Step 1 and the bottom left edge as a guide. Flip your model.

(continued)

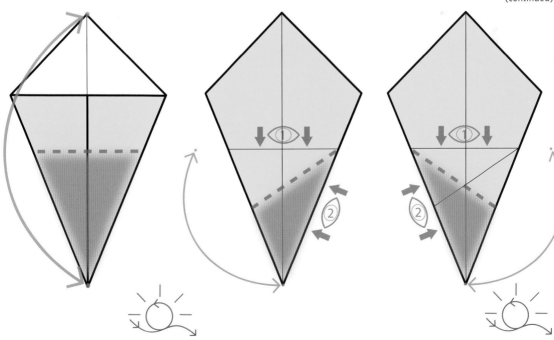

Folding the Roosting Robin *continued*

4 Lift your model off your work surface and fold only the top area in half vertically. You will find that the bottom area pivots and automatically produces an outside reverse fold from the folds you made in Steps 2 and 3.

5 Your model should look like this. Fold the left tip down and toward the right, as shown, to form the bird's head.

6 Outside reverse fold the fold you made in Step 5 to complete your model.

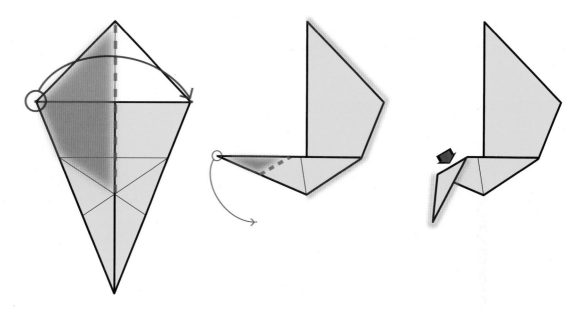

Your completed roosting robin should look like this.

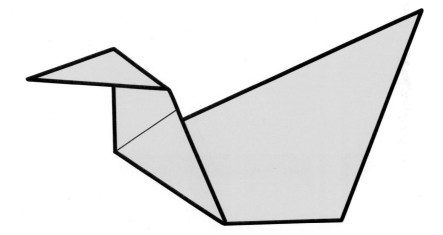

New Symbol: Reverse Fold

Symbol Icon

▬ ▬ ▬ ▬ ▬ ▬

Whenever you see a blue dashed line, you will need to perform a reverse fold. In this example, if we reverse two folds, we will obtain a flap. Flaps are useful for folding things like legs, flippers, feet, and arms. It is very important to remember to use your fingernail or a tool to sharpen folds before reversing them. Sharp folds reverse easily, dull ones do not.

1. This step calls for reversing two folds, which will result in the left corner moving up and to the center.

2. This diagram shows these folds as they are now. The valley fold (green dashed line) needs to become a mountain fold. The mountain fold (red dotted and dashed line) needs to become a valley fold.

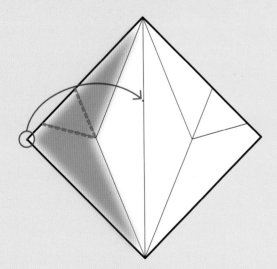

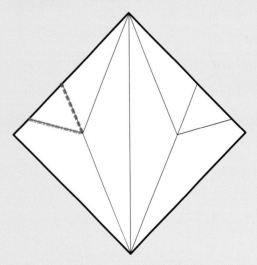

(continued)

New Symbol: Reverse Fold continued

3. Valley Fold to Mountain Fold

Lift your paper and slide the tip of your index finger of one hand under the fold to be reversed while at the same time lightly pinching the paper with your other hand.

4. Mountain Fold to Valley Fold

Flip your paper and do the same procedure for the second fold.

After completion of these two reverse folds, your paper should have a flap on it.

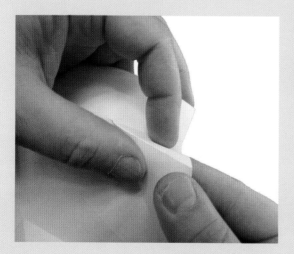

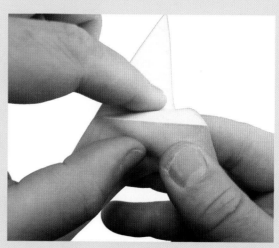

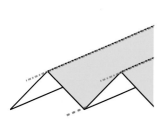

Remember: Green valleys and red mountaintops.

Folding the Tropical Fish

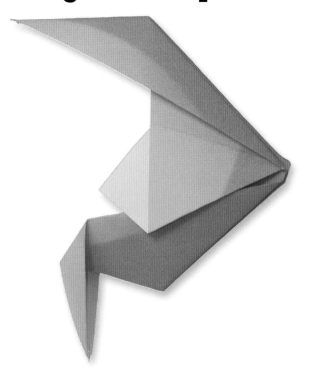

1 Begin with the kite shape (page 14). Fold and then unfold both upper edges to the center fold.

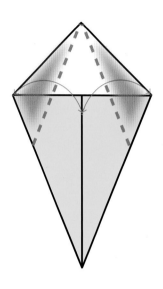

2 Unfold the kite shape.

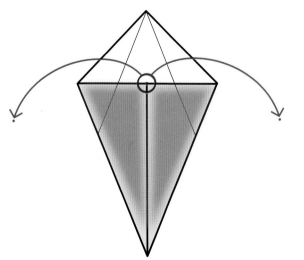

3 Reverse the folds highlighted in blue, and then fold the outside corners to the center as shown. This will create two new flaps.

(continued)

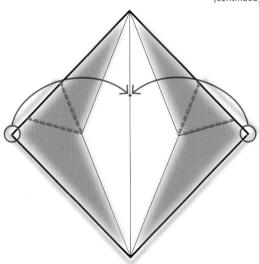

Folding the Tropical Fish continued

4 Your model should look like this. Flip it.

5 Fold your model in half vertically.

6 Your paper should look like this.

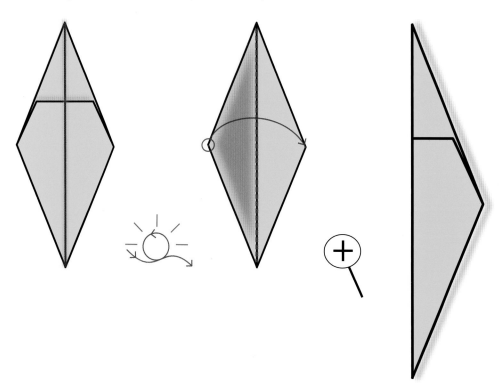

New Symbol: Magnifying Glass

Symbol Icon

When you see this symbol, the size of the model in the diagrams increases. As we fold a model, it gets smaller and folding symbols become tiny. This allows the model to look larger on the page so symbols are more clear.

7 Fold the bottom tip along the fold line shown in the diagram.

Start the fold a little bit below this corner.

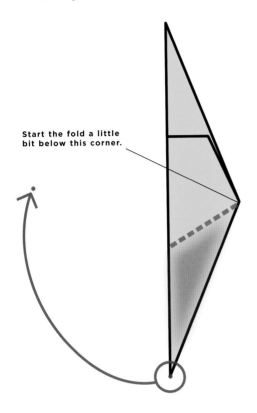

8 Outside reverse fold the fold you made in Step 7.

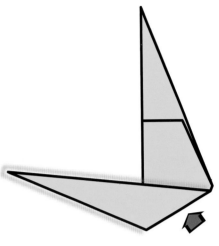

9 Fold the left-most tip down as shown.

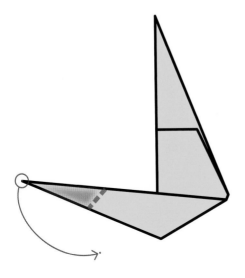

10 Outside reverse fold the fold you made in Step 9.

(continued)

Folding the Tropical Fish continued

11 Fold the flap down as shown in the diagram. Flip your model and do the same on the other side.

12 Fold the top tip down at an angle as shown in the diagram.

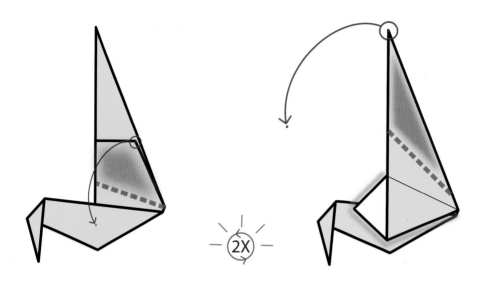

13 Outside reverse fold the fold you made in Step 12.

Your completed tropical fish should look like this.

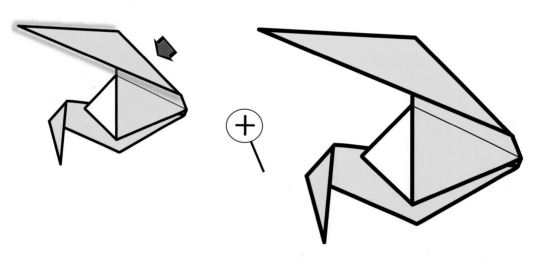

New Symbol: Fold on Both Sides

Symbol Icon

Just like the flip symbol, the fold on both sides symbol is easily overlooked, but this mistake is usually discovered soon after. The symbol's meaning is simple: repeat the same fold you just did on the other side of the model.

1. Fold the flap down as indicated.

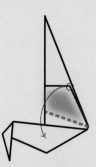

2. Your model should look like this. Flip it.

3. Fold the flap down as indicated.

4. Your model will look like this. Flip it back to its original position before going to the next step.

In Step 11 on the previous page, our intention was to add pectoral fins to both sides of our fish. Notice how the fold on both sides symbol simplifies this sequence of diagrams. The key point to remember when you see this symbol is to perform exactly the same fold as you did in the diagram associated with it, but on the other side of the model.

Other Things You Can Do

Notice that this model uses color from both sides of the paper. This means you can make a two-colored fish by coloring each side of your square with a different color.

If you make a few of these fish, you can make a mobile to hang from the ceiling.

These fish were folded from the blue, red, and yellow paper that comes with this book. If you do decide to make some fish from these squares, make sure you save some paper for the origami flower presented later in this book.

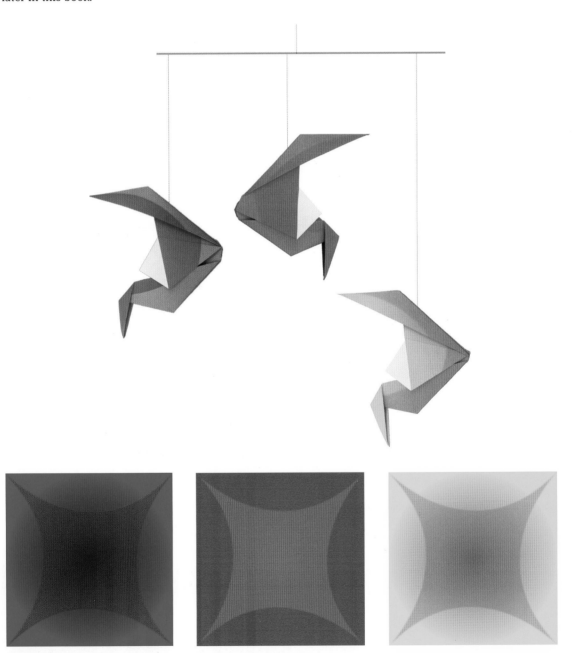

Folding the Parakeet

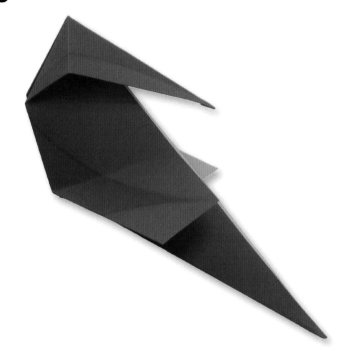

1 Fold the kite shape
(page 14).

2 Fold the tropical fish (page 39) through
Step 4. Fold and then unfold the bottom tip up
to the right outside corner as shown.

(continued)

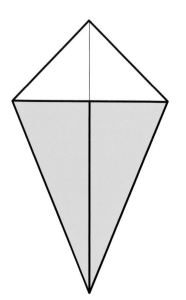

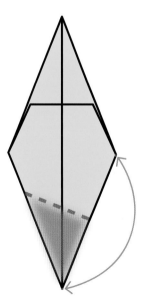

Folding the Parakeet continued

3 Fold and then unfold the bottom tip up and to the left outside corner as shown and then flip your model.

4 Lift your model off your work surface and fold only the top portion in half vertically as shown. You will find that an outside reverse fold forms automatically in the lower portion.

5 Your model should look like this. Push the left tip toward the center of the model to add a bit of shape to the head. Reorient your model.

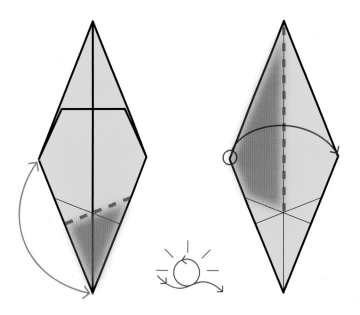

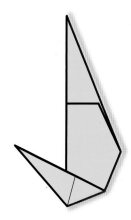

Your completed parakeet should look like this.

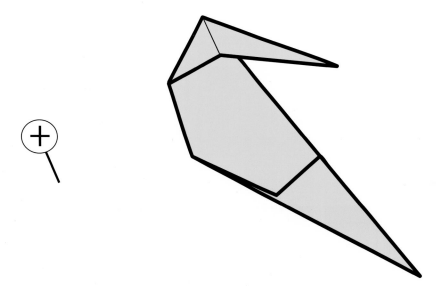

Folding the Peacock

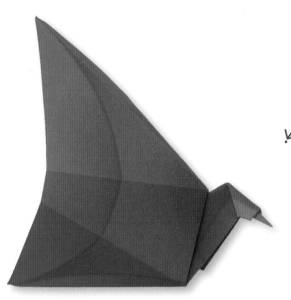

1 Begin with the kite shape (page 14) and then unfold it. Reorient your paper as shown in the next diagram.

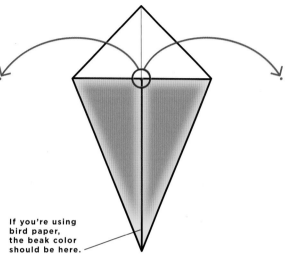

If you're using bird paper, the beak color should be here.

2 Fold and then unfold the square in half.

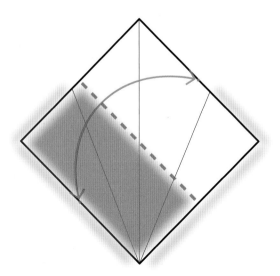

3 Fold and then unfold the square in half in the other direction.

(continued)

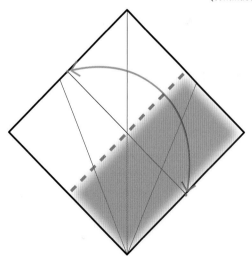

Folding the Peacock continued

4 Fold your square back into the kite shape.

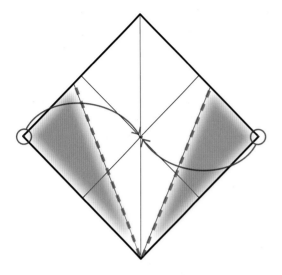

5 Your model should look like this. Flip it.

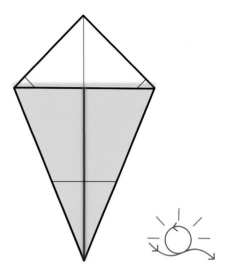

6 Fold the bottom tip up as shown. Note that the fold is made horizontally where two diagonal folds intersect the edge of the paper.

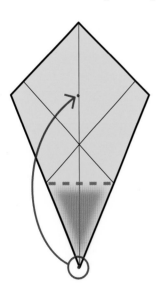

7A Pinch fold at the points indicated in the diagram. You want to work your fingers between these layers of paper.

(continued)

This tip moves away from you.

Mountain fold

This tip moves toward you.

New Symbol: Zoom Window

Symbol Icon

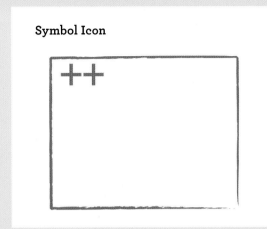

As we fold a model, its overall size tends to become smaller. Sometimes we will need to do small, detailed folding on a specific area of the model. If we kept that area the same size as in previous steps, the folding symbols would become illegibly small.

The zoom window is a box that identifies the portion of the model enlarged in subsequent diagrams. No folds will occur outside this window while it is active.

1. The zoom window as it appears on a diagram

2. This change in scale will end as soon as you see a diagram that contains the complete model.

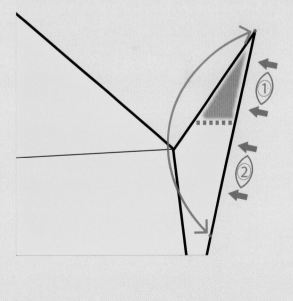

Folding the Peacock continued

7B Notice that I use the index finger of my left hand to support the mountain fold as I perform the pinch fold with my right hand.

8A Crush fold the bottom of your model so it becomes flat again.

8B Your model should look like this. Now we will fold the peacock's head.

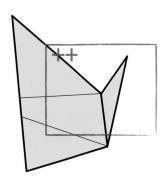

9 Fold and then unfold the narrow tip down, using the edge of your paper as a guide.

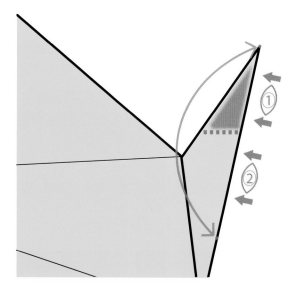

10 Fold and then unfold the narrow tip using the upper edge of the paper (alignment symbol 1) and the fold you made in Step 9 (alignment symbol 2) as guides.

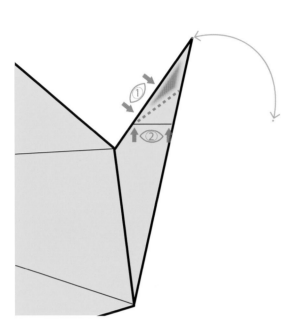

11 Perform a T-fold on the folds you made in Steps 9 and 10.

(continued)

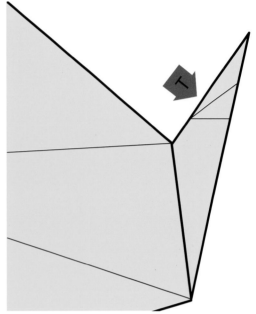

New Symbol: T-Fold

Symbol Icon

T-folds are useful for making shapes like animal heads. When a T-fold is needed, you will see a red arrow with a "T" inside it. The arrow points at the area where the T-fold will be performed. A T-fold is accomplished by partially opening your model and manipulating two folds you made in the two steps before the T-fold symbol.

(continued)

New Symbol: T-Fold continued

1. Notice that the T-fold symbol is pointing toward two fold lines, one horizontal and one diagonal. These folds were made in the two steps preceding this one.

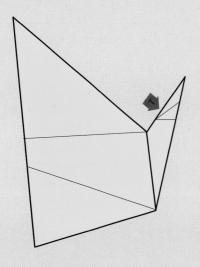

2. Gently open the two layers of paper affected by the folds.

3. Pinch the layers you opened in Step 2 while you push the tip down. The layers of paper encompassing the tip will wrap around the layers you're pinching.

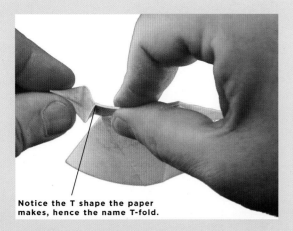

Notice the T shape the paper makes, hence the name T-fold.

4. Pinch the area you just folded to secure the folds. *NOTE: Some books refer to this fold as a crimp fold.*

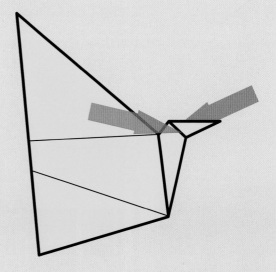

Folding the Peacock continued

12 Open the top layer of paper on the bird's head.

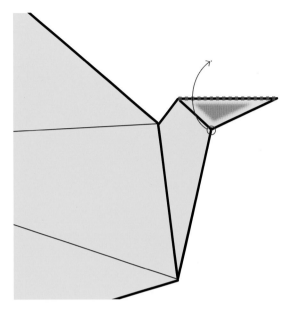

13 Fold the tip of the beak to the back of the neck.

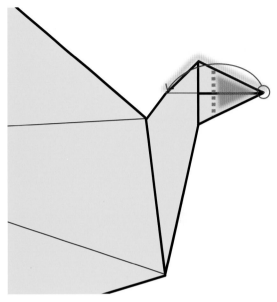

14 Fold the tip of the beak as shown, leaving a gap between the fold you're making now and the one you made in Step 13.

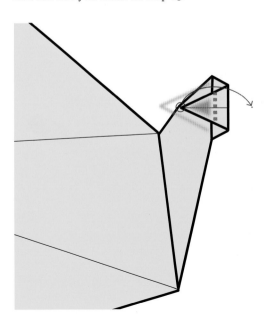

15 Fold the flap you folded in Step 12 back down. Pinch the area to ensure the folds you made in Steps 13 and 14 stay in place.

(continued)

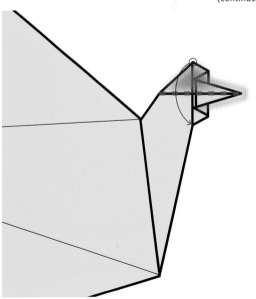

Folding the Peacock continued

16 Pull open the large flap in the rear.

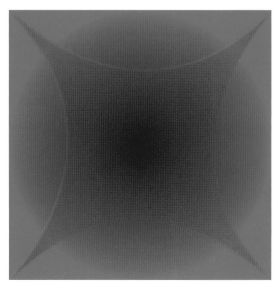

Here are two views of a peacock I made with the blue paper that comes with this book.

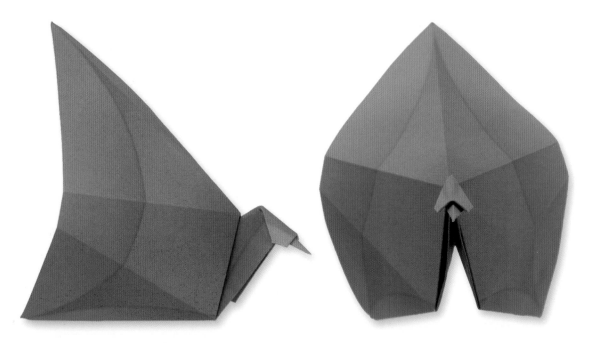

Folding the Baby Seal

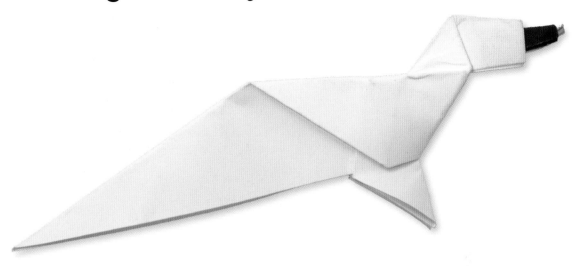

1 Fold the kite shape (page 14).

2 Fold the tropical fish (page 39) through Step 6.

3 Fold the large flap down as shown, on both sides of your model.

(continued)

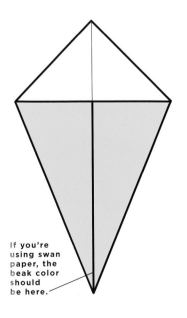

If you're using swan paper, the beak color should be here.

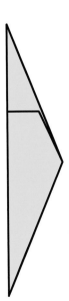

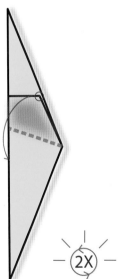

2X

Folding the Baby Seal continued

4 Fold the small flap up as shown. Flip your model and repeat on the other side.

5 Your model should look like this.

6 Fold the top layer of the right lower edge, aligning it with the left edge. Flip your model and do the same on the other side.

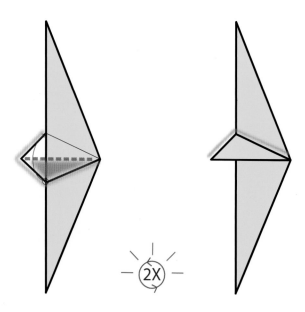

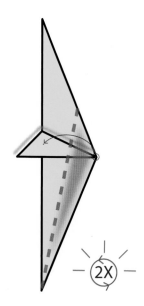

7 Reorient your model as shown. Fold the narrow tip up. Start the fold a little bit to the right of the edge of the flap that sticks out from the bottom.

8 Your model should look like this. Inside reverse fold the fold you made in Step 7.

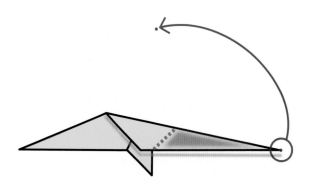

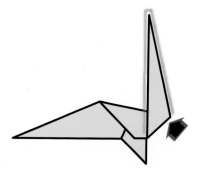

9 Fold the tip down as shown.

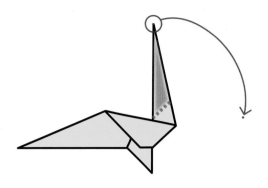

10 Inside reverse fold the fold you made in Step 9.

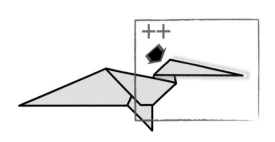

11 Fold the top layer of paper down as shown in the diagram.

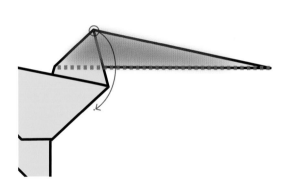

12A Fold the top in half vertically as shown in the diagram.

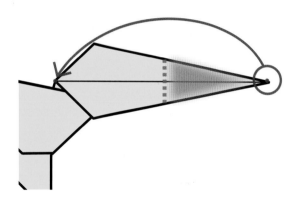

13A Close the fold you opened in Step 11.

Your model should look like this. Spread the front flippers and your seal should stand on its own.

(continued)

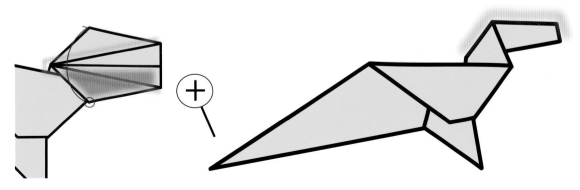

For a More Detailed Head

Experienced folders can add a snout and tiny nose to your baby seal model. Instead of folding the head in half in Step 12A, do the following:

12B Fold the tip to the left as shown in the diagram (much further than you did in Step 12A).

13B Fold the tip to the right as shown in the diagram.

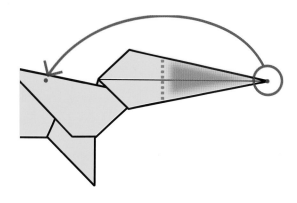

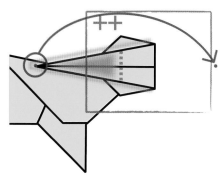

14 Fold the tip to the left as shown in the diagram.

15 Fold the tip to the right again as shown in the diagram.

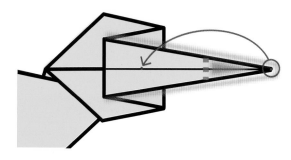

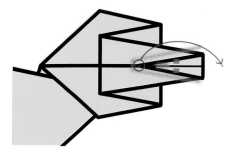

16 Fold what is remaining of the tip to the left to form a tiny nose.

17 Fold the bottom corner of the head up along the fold line you unfolded in Step 11.

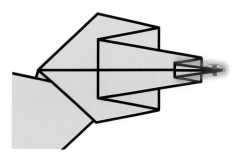

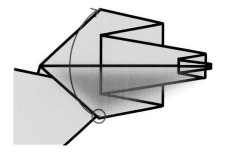

Your model should look like this. Spread the front flippers so your seal will stand on its own.

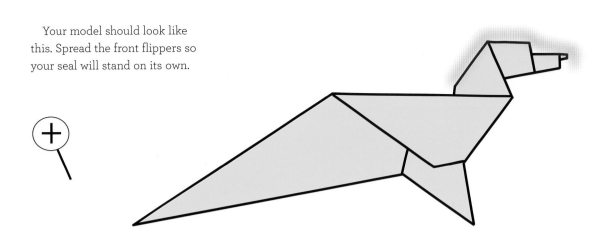

Other Things You Can Do

In Steps 9 and 10 you can make a T-fold rather than an inside reverse fold to obtain a different head shape.

Try using swan paper to make the baby seal model. It will result in a white seal with a black snout and orange nose. When using swan paper, make sure you fold the kite shape with the beak color on the narrower tip.

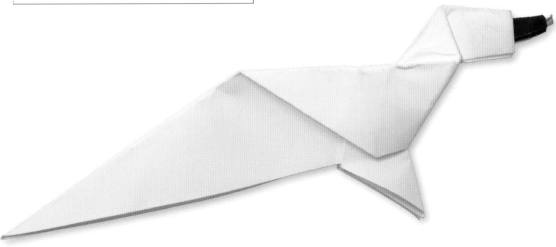

Folding the Chick

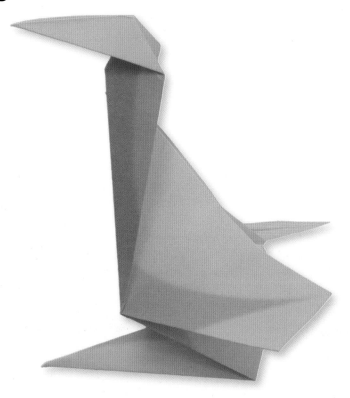

1 Fold the kite shape
(page 14).

2 Fold the tropical fish (page 39) through
Step 4. Fold and then unfold your model in
half horizontally and then flip it.

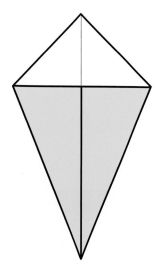

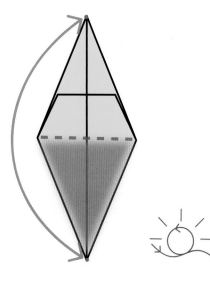

3 Fold only the top layer of paper on this and the next step.

Fold and then unfold the top tip down and to the left using the right upper edge and the fold you made in Step 2 as a guide.

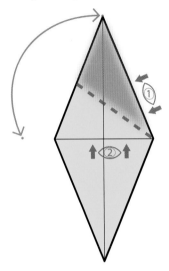

4 Fold and then unfold the top tip down and to the right using the left upper edge and the fold you made in Step 2 as a guide.

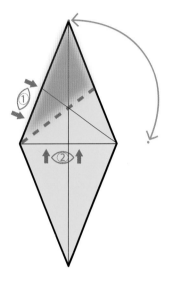

5 Fold only the area shown in half vertically on the existing fold. You will find that the top tip will lift off your work surface and an inside reverse fold will form from the folds you made in Steps 3 and 4.

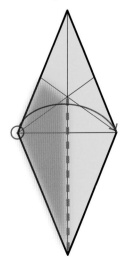

6 Your model should look like this. Fold the bottom corner up and to the left as shown.
(continued)

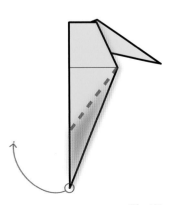

Folding the Chick continued

7 Your model should look like this. Outside reverse fold the fold you made in Step 6.

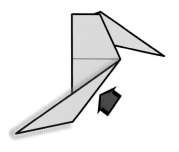

8 Fold the bottom tip to the right as shown.

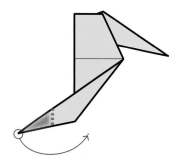

9 Outside reverse fold the fold you made in Step 8.

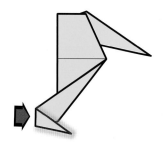

Reorient your model, and your completed chick should look like this.

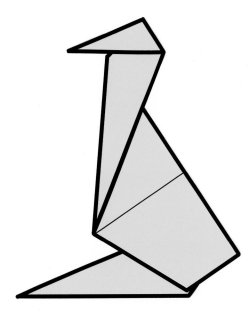

Folding the Simple Swan

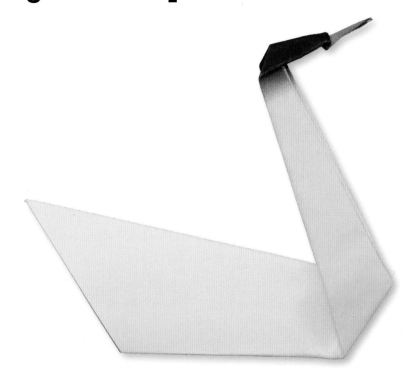

1 Begin with the kite shape (page 14). Fold each edge to the center fold as shown.

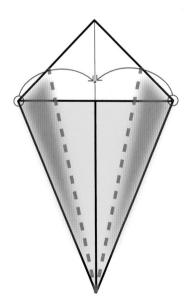

2 Your model should look like this. Fold it in half vertically as shown.

(continued)

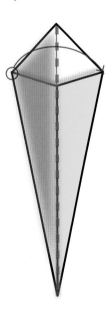

Folding the Simple Swan continued

3 Fold and then unfold your model in half horizontally as shown in the diagram. We will use this fold as a reference when folding the neck of the swan in the next step.

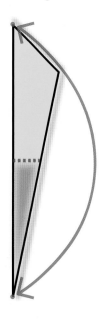

4 Reorient your model as shown. Fold the narrow tip up and back at an angle. You want your swan's neck to arc backwards in a graceful manner. Look at the next diagram if you need to.

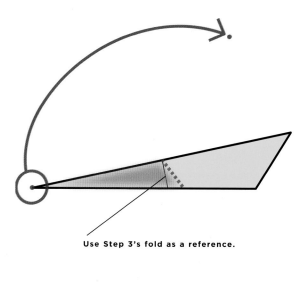

Use Step 3's fold as a reference.

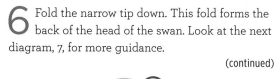

5 Your model should look like this. Outside reverse fold the fold you made in Step 4.

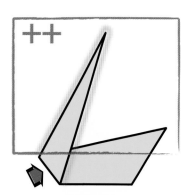

6 Fold the narrow tip down. This fold forms the back of the head of the swan. Look at the next diagram, 7, for more guidance.

(continued)

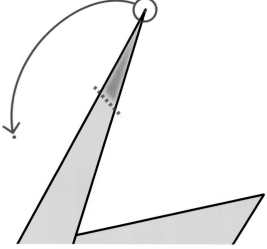

New Symbol: Zoom to a View

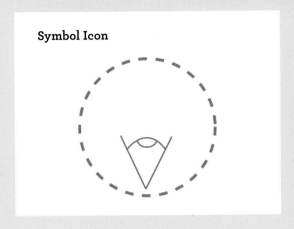

Symbol Icon

The zoom to a view symbol allows us to change the perspective of a group of diagrams that follow it. In order to do this, you have to temporarily open a portion of the model being folded. This opening allows us to peek inside and make some additional folds.

1. In this example, our goal is to open the swan's head and add a beak. In order to show this in diagrams, we need to change the perspective.

The zoom to a view symbol not only changes the perspective, but it will direct you to open a fold in order to reveal a surface that is not visible.

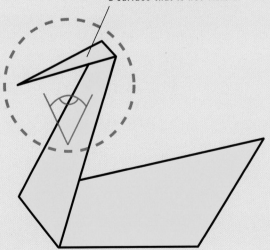

2. Here is the next diagram in the sequence. Now the underside of the swan's head is visible and can be folded. When you see the entire model again, the zoom to a view has ended and diagrams will proceed normally.

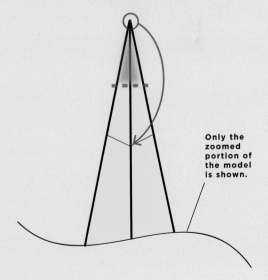

Only the zoomed portion of the model is shown.

Folding the Simple Swan continued

7 Outside reverse fold the fold you made in Step 6.

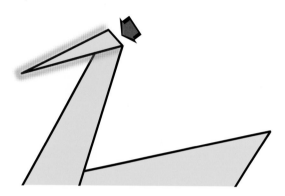

8 Your model should look like this. In order to fold the beak, we will need to open the head of the swan. The next diagrams are the view you would have if looking at the underside of the unfolded head.

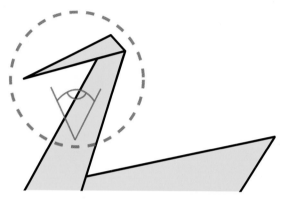

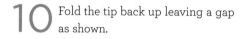

9 We are now looking at the underside of the opened head. Fold the tip down to the fold you made in Step 6.

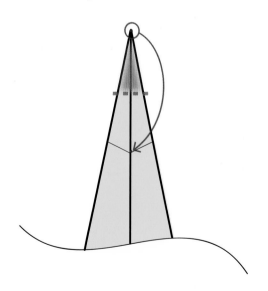

10 Fold the tip back up leaving a gap as shown.

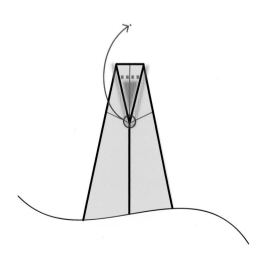

11 The head of your model should look like this. Refold the outside reverse fold you made in Step 7 and…

…your completed swan should look like this. Once you have practiced this model a few times, you might want to try the more complex swan on page 75.

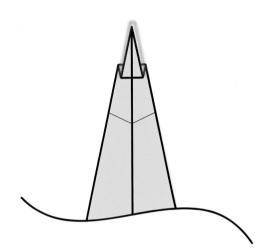

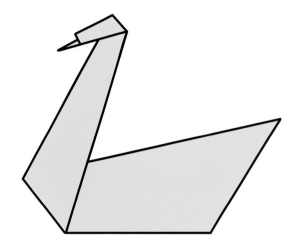

Other Things You Can Do

It is only necessary to make the fold in Step 3 as a reference. Once you have folded a swan, you can try moving the fold in Step 4 to the left or right to change the swan's proportions.

The fold in Step 4 determines whether the swan's neck is swept back or forward or anything in between. You can make a bunch of swans in different poses by making the fold in Step 4 at different angles.

The fold in Step 6 determines whether the swan is looking up or down. The more your swan's head points down, the more graceful it will appear.

The swan pictured below was made with paper that comes with this book (pictured below). Once you have successfully completed the swan with practice paper, you might consider making one.

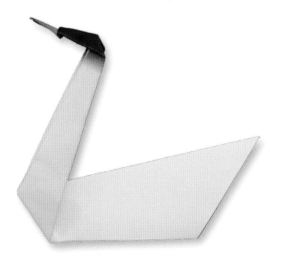

Folding the Sitting Dragon

1 Fold the kite shape (page 14).

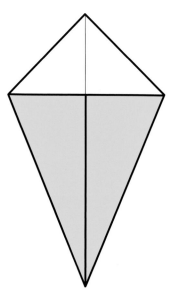

2 Fold the tropical fish (page 39) through Step 6.

3 Fold the baby seal (page 55) through Step 3.

4 Fold the top layer of the lower right edge aligning it with the left edge. Flip your model and repeat on the other side.

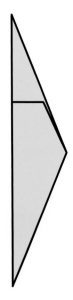

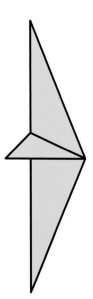

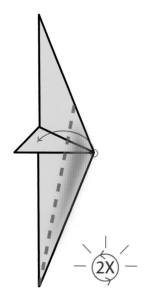

2X

5 Fold the top layer of the right upper edge aligning it with the left edge. Flip your model and repeat on the other side.

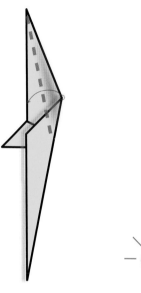

6 Your model should look like this.

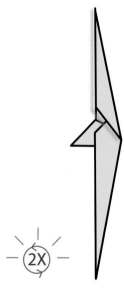

— ↻ 2X ↺ —

7 Fold the top tip down, at an angle.

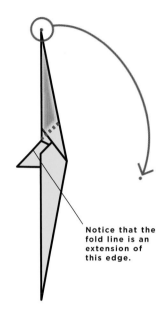

Notice that the fold line is an extension of this edge.

8 Your model should look like this. Inside reverse fold the fold you made in Step 7.

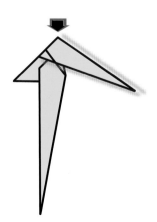

9 Fold the tip on the right up at an angle. This fold will form the head of your dragon. You can make your dragon look up or down depending on the angle of this fold.

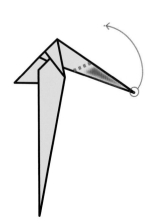

10 Inside reverse fold the fold you made in Step 9.

(continued)

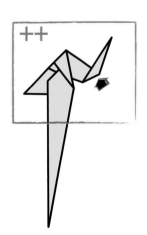

Folding the Sitting Dragon continued

11 Unfold the top layer of paper as shown

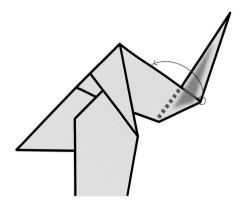

12 Fold the tip down as shown.

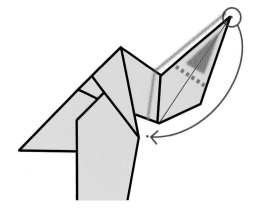

13 Close the fold you opened in Step 11.

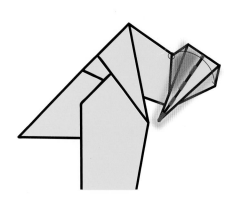

14 Fold the bottom tip up and toward the left as shown.

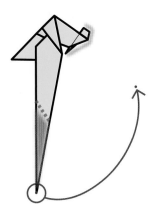

15 Inside reverse fold the fold you made in Step 14.

16 Fold the tip down as shown and then inside reverse fold it.

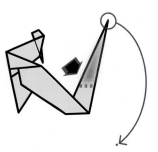

17 Fold the tip up as shown and then inside reverse fold it.

Your completed sitting dragon should look like this.

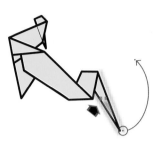

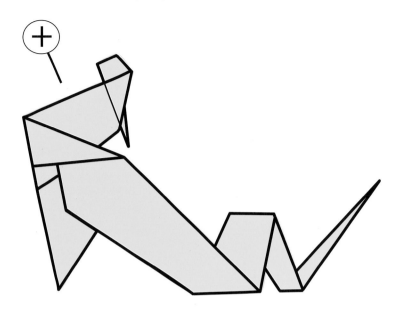

Other Things You Can Do

Once you've completed the dragon model successfully, try folding one from the dark green origami paper provided with this book. You can make many modifications to this folding pattern. Try changing the head shape in Steps 9 through 13. Change the angles of the tail in Steps 14 through 17.

The sitting dragon photo below was folded using the green pattern paper that comes with this book.

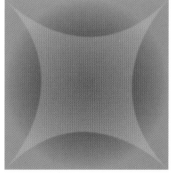

Folding the Snail

1 Begin by folding the kite shape (page 14). Reorient it such that the narrow point is at the top. Fold and then unfold the bottom right edge up and to the left using the bottom left edge for alignment as shown.

2 Fold and then unfold the bottom left edge up and to the right using the bottom right edge for alignment as shown. Flip your model.

3 Fold and then unfold the bottom corner up as shown and then flip your model.

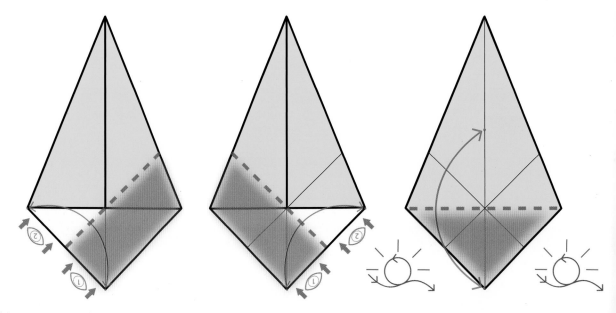

4 Fold each of the outside corners up and toward the center on the existing folds. This will create a flap on the lower end of your model.

5 Your model should look like this. Fold the outside corners of the top layer of paper down and to the center as shown.

6 Inside reverse fold the folds you made in Step 5.

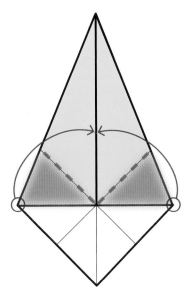

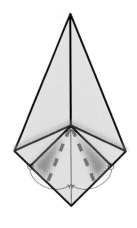

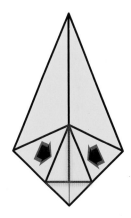

7 Fold the inner narrow tip of the top layer down.

8 Fold the right corner of the top layer to the left along the existing fold line.

9 Your model should look like this. Flip it.

(continued)

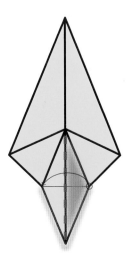

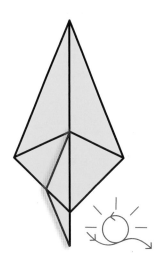

Folding the Snail continued

10 Fold the top layer of paper in half vertically as shown.

11 Fold the left edge to the right as shown. Flip your model and repeat on the other side.

12 Fold the narrow tip down and to the right. You can feel where to make this fold as it is just ahead of the thickest area of paper.

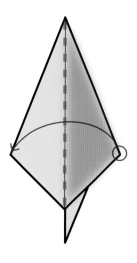

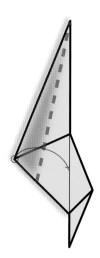

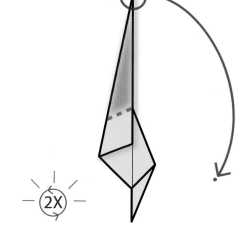

13 Outside reverse fold the fold you made in Step 12.

14 Fold the narrow tip up and to the left as shown.

15 Outside reverse fold the fold you made in Step 14.

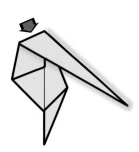

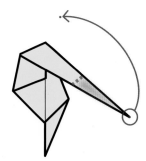

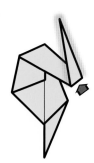

16 Fold the upper tip down and to the left as shown.

17 Outside reverse fold the fold you made in Step 16.

18 Fold the upper tip to the left as shown.

19 Outside reverse fold the fold you made in Step 18.

Your completed snail should look like this. Spread the tail for a slimier look.

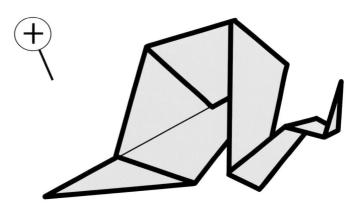

Folding the Graceful Swan

TIP This model is a combination of conventional origami and pinch folding. Watching the video of this model is suggested.

1 Begin with the kite shape (page 14). Fold each edge to the center fold as shown.

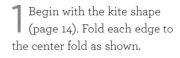

If you're using swan paper, start with the beak color here.

2 Fold each edge to the center fold again.

3 Your model should look like this. Fold and then unfold your model in half horizontally, and then flip it.

4 Fold your model in half vertically and then reorient it so it looks like the next diagram.

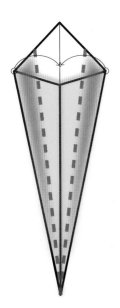

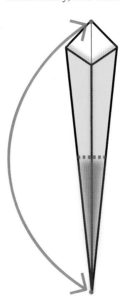

5 Fold the narrow tip up and to the left as shown to form the swan's neck.

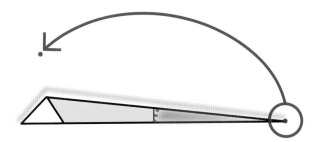

6 Inside reverse fold the fold you made in Step 5.

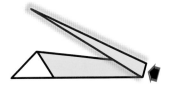

7 Pinch the fold you made in Step 6 while you push the paper up and around the swan's neck with your other fingers. Work the paper, and don't be bashful about pushing with a fair amount of force.

8 Pinch the fold you made in Step 6 while you pull out the inner layers of paper from inside of the swan's body.

(continued)

Folding the Graceful Swan continued

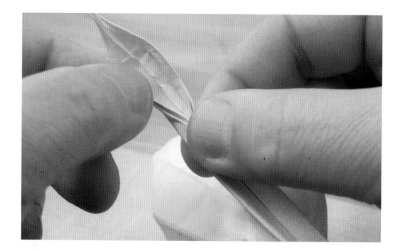

9 Open all except the bottom two layers of paper inside the narrow tip (the swan's head). Pinch the neck just below the area you're opening to keep it from opening too.

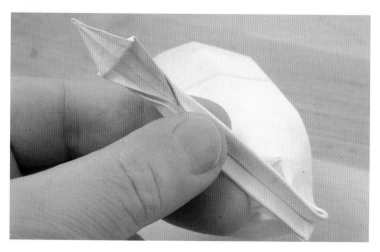

10 Fold the tip down, and then back up leaving a small gap to form the swan's beak.

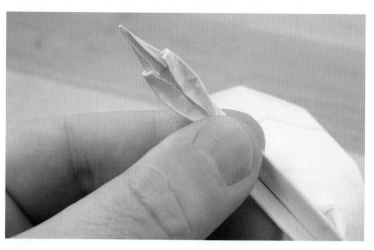

11 Narrow the beak by folding the edges to the center and then crush folding the pockets that form.

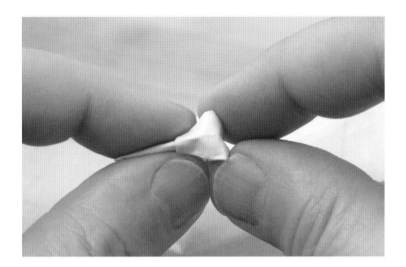

12 Pinch the head into a swan-like shape.

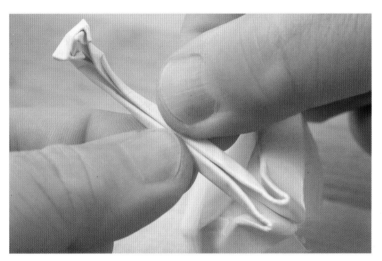

13 Pinch the neck, rounding its edges, and then add a graceful curve to the length of it.

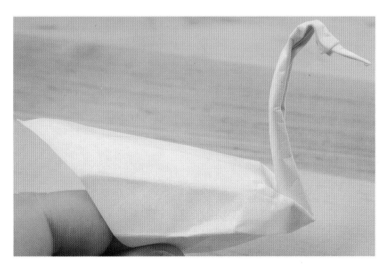

Your completed graceful swan should look like this.

The Collapsed Square

The collapsed square is fairly easy to fold and will allow you to fold many more models. The collapsed square and the collapsed triangle are made from the same folding pattern, but yield very different shapes.

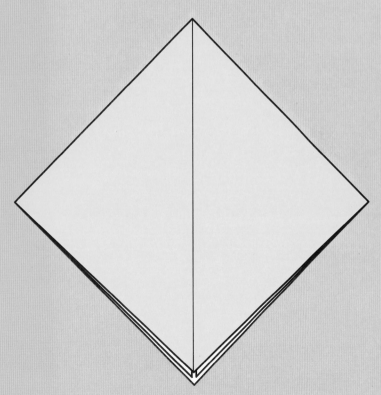

Folding the Collapsed Square

1 For most models you will begin with the colored side of the paper facing up.

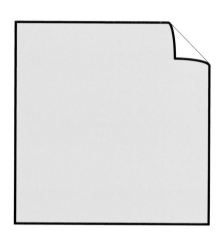

2 Fold and then unfold your square in half diagonally.

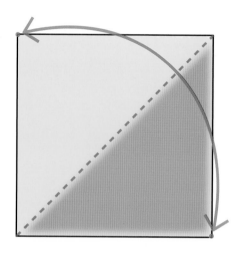

3 Fold and then unfold your square in half on the other diagonal and then flip your paper.

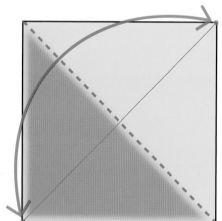

4 Fold and then unfold your square in half horizontally.

(continued)

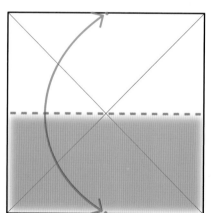

New Symbol: Collapse

Symbol Icon

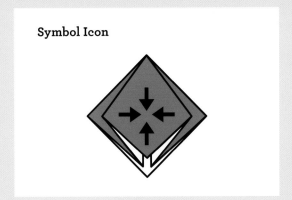

Collapse folds require some practice, but are becoming common in origami diagrams. They're hard to understand at first because the change they make to our paper is so radical. With a little practice, you will master this technique and perform these folds with ease.

1. The collapse fold symbol always appears along with a diagram showing mountain and valley folds that are already on your paper. The technique is simple-pinch the mountain folds and the valley folds will automatically move where they need to.

2. Lightly pinch the mountain folds near the outer edges of your square as you gently push toward the center. You should see the center of the square begin to lift off your work surface. The following pictures show this movement in more detail.

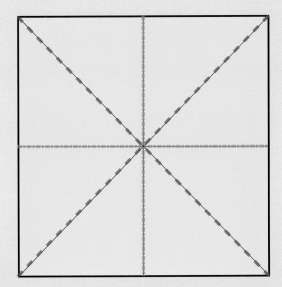

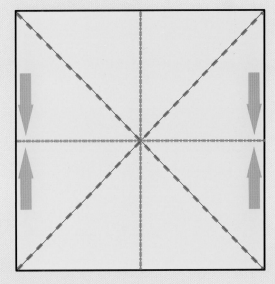

(continued)

New Symbol: Collapse continued

3. Allow the center to rise while applying light pressure both down and toward the center.

4. Continue pushing toward the center.

5. Lift and complete the movement toward the center.

6. The last step is to make sure you have an even number of pleats of paper on both sides, and to run your finger over the folds to secure them.

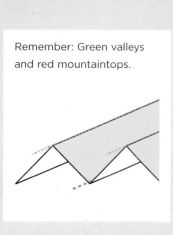

Remember: Green valleys and red mountaintops.

Your completed collapsed square should look like this.

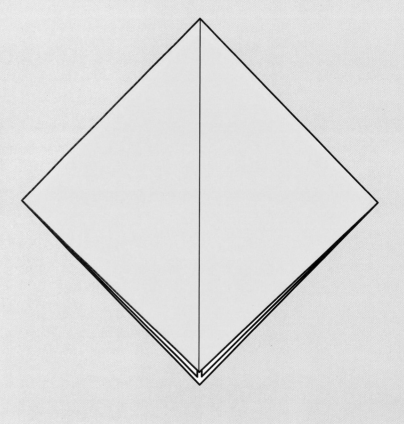

Folding the Collapsed Square *continued*

5 Fold and then unfold your square vertically. Flip your paper.

6 Your paper should look like this. Notice that the diagonals are valley folds and the horizontal and vertical are mountain folds. Now perform a collapse fold.

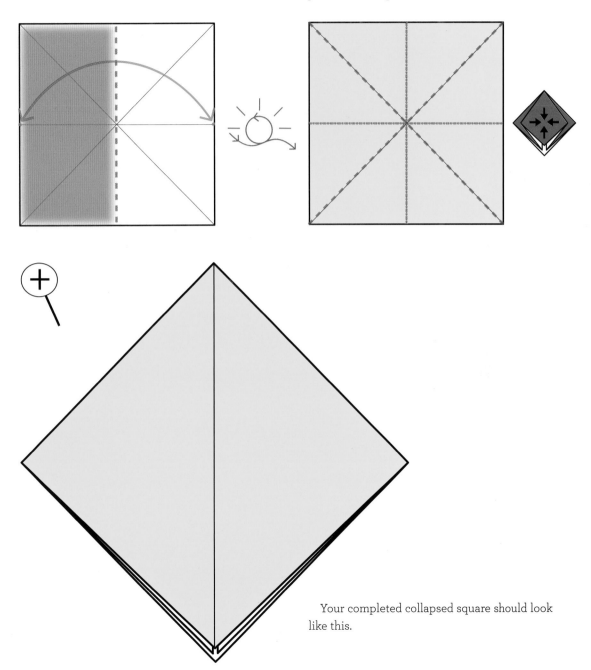

Your completed collapsed square should look like this.

Folding the Crocus

1 Begin by folding a collapsed square (page 82), starting with the colored side of the square facing down.

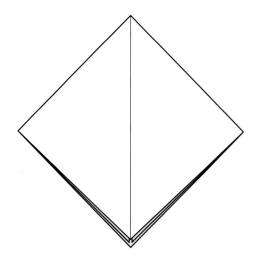

2 Fold the top layer's bottom corner to the top. Flip your model and do the same on the other side.

3 Your model should look like this. Book fold your model to reveal the unfolded layers of paper.

(continued)

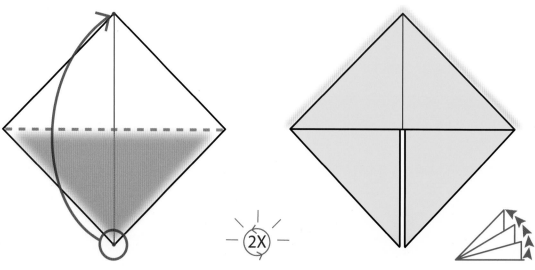

New Symbol: Book Fold

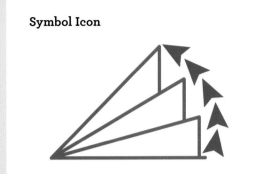

Symbol Icon

A book fold allows us to perform folds on layers of paper that are inside the model. When you see this symbol, it means you need to fold one side of the top layer of paper much like you would turn the pages of a book. This fold is easily mastered and has great potential.

1. Fold the right corner of the top layer in half vertically on the existing fold and then flip your model.

2. Fold the right corner of the top layer in half vertically again.

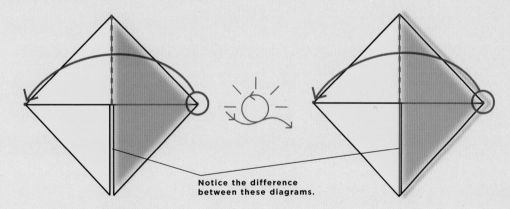

Notice the difference between these diagrams.

3. Your model should look like this.

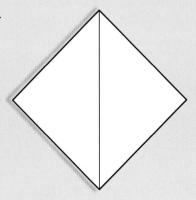

(continued)

New Symbol: Book Fold continued

When you encounter the book fold symbol in the future, the series of steps will look like this:

1. Book fold your model.

2. Your model should look like this.

Folding the Crocus continued

4 Fold the top layer as you did in Step 2. Flip your model and do the same on the other side.

5 Your model should look like this. Completely unfold it.

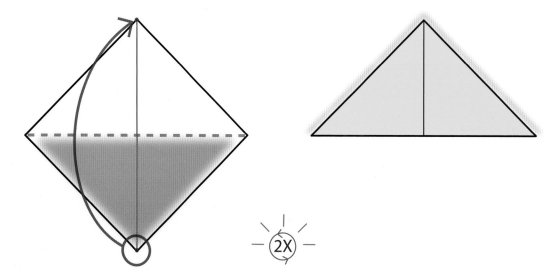

6 With the colored side facing up, fold and then unfold the top and bottom edges to the center.

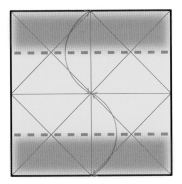

7 Fold and then unfold the left and right edges to the center.

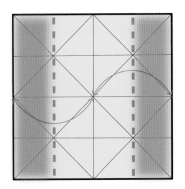

8A Fold the center point of each side to the center of the square. Allow the flaps this creates to move freely while doing this. Look at the pictures that follow to gain a better understanding of how the paper is moving.

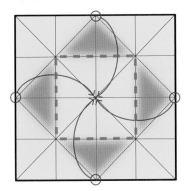

8B I use my thumbs and index fingers to push the triangles into place.

8C Push each of the flaps down so they lie flat.

8D Your model should look like this.

(continued)

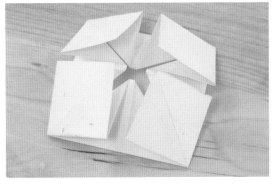

Folding the Crocus continued

9 Notice that the top layer of your model has four small squares. Each small square has a flap with a corner in the center. Flip your model.

10 Fold the bottom corner to the center, but lift your model slightly to allow the loose flap on the bottom to rotate to the outside of the model. In other words, do not fold the loose flap on the bottom.

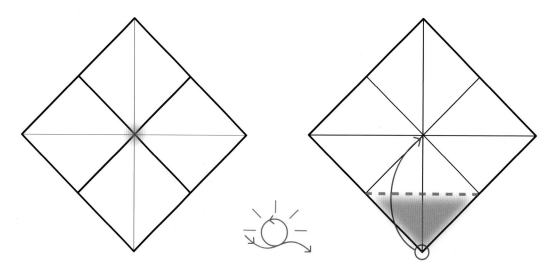

11 Your model will look like this. Perform the same fold on the other three corners of your model.

12 Your model will look like this. Flip it.

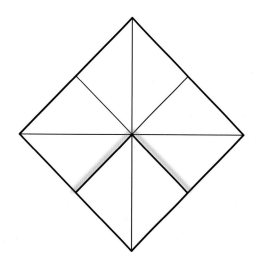

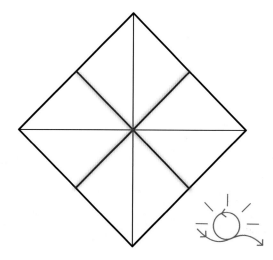

13 Now we will shape the flower. Insert the index finger of your left hand into the center, and lift one of the top flaps. Insert the index finger and thumb of your right hand into the pockets that form. Now remove the index finger of your left hand from the flap and squeeze with your right index finger and thumb. Perform the same procedure for the other three center flaps.

14 Insert your fingers as shown and squeeze toward the center.

15 Insert your fingers as deep as you can into the petals and squeeze to the center to complete shaping of your flower. When you release it, you'll have a crocus!

Other Things You Can Do

Now you know how to fold both leaves and flowers, so you can make a plant in bloom!

Folding the Rambunctious Dog

1 Fold the collapsed square (page 82).

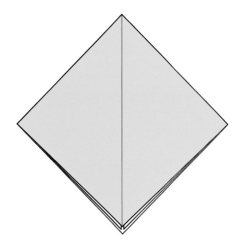

2 Fold the crocus (page 86) through Step 8.

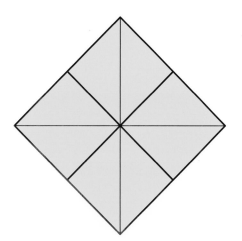

3 Open and fold the left and right inside corners down to the bottom (look at the next diagram).

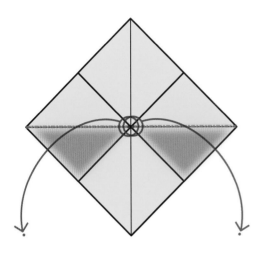

4 Your model should look like this. Flip it.

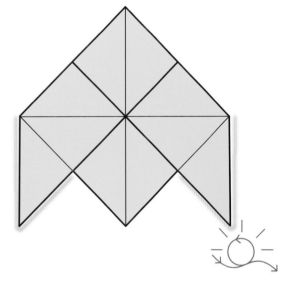

5 Fold the outer corners toward the middle using the bottom edges for alignment as shown.

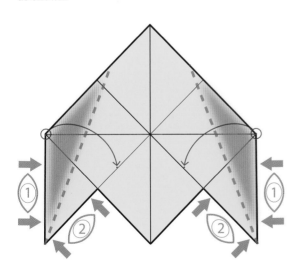

6 Your model should look like this. Flip it.

(continued)

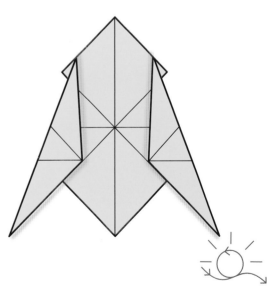

Folding the Rambunctious Dog continued

7 Fold the corners of the top two layers of paper to the center fold as shown.

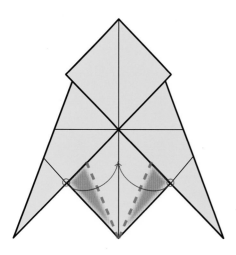

8 Inside reverse fold the two folds you made in Step 7. This will create a flap. Flip your model.

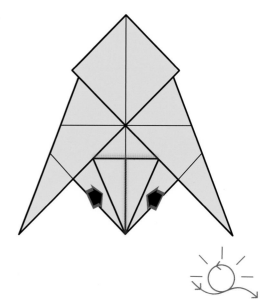

9 Fold the bottom corner up to the center point, allowing the flap you created in Step 8 to rotate to the outside of the model.

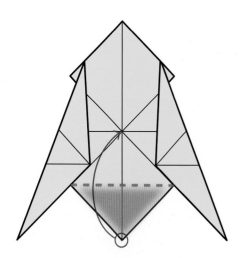

10 Your model should look like this. Flip it and then...

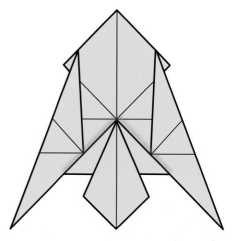

11 …crush fold the flaps as shown.

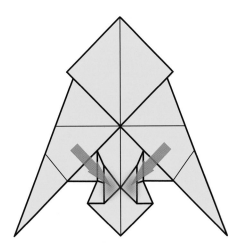

12 Fold your model in half vertically and reorient it so it looks like the next diagram.

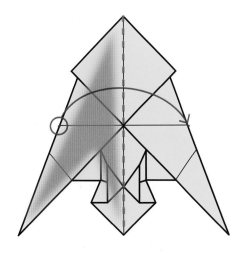

13 Push the dog's nose down and pinch fold the back of his head to complete your model.

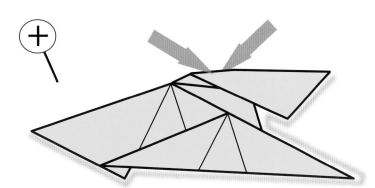

Other Things You Can Do

You can adjust whether your rambunctious dogs are lying down or running by extending or retracting the rear-most flap of paper.

Folding the Eight-Pointed Star

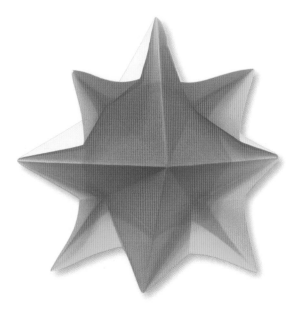

1 Begin by folding the collapsed square, (page 82), starting with the colored side of the paper facing up.

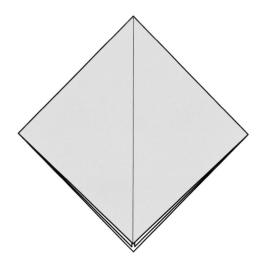

2 Fold the crocus (page 86) through Step 8 and then completely unfold it. Flip your square.

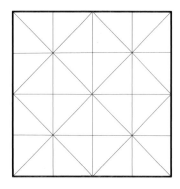

3 Reverse the left and right inner vertical folds by folding, sharpening the fold by running your finger along it, and then unfolding.

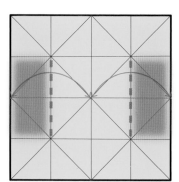

4 Reverse the upper and lower inner horizontal folds by folding, sharpening the fold by running your finger along it, and then unfolding.

5A Pinch two opposing corners and push them toward the center. Do the same with the other two corners. See the pictures that follow for clarification.

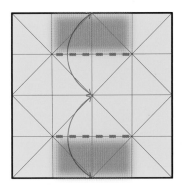

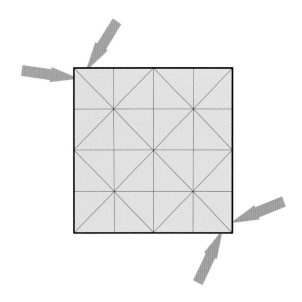

5B I have pinched two opposite corners and am pushing them gently toward the center of the model.

5C I do the same with the other two corners.

(continued)

Folding the Eight-Pointed Star *continued*

6A Shape your model by pinching two opposite lower points and pushing gently toward the center of the model.

6B Now do the same with the other two lower points.

Your completed eight-pointed star should look like this.

Other Things You Can Do

Eight-pointed stars make great decorations. With a needle and thread you can make a nifty hanger for your stars and decorate wreaths, Christmas trees, or just about anything.

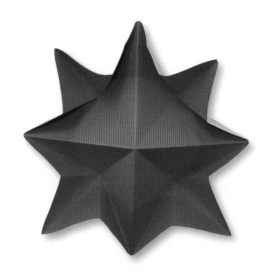

Folding the Ornamental Box

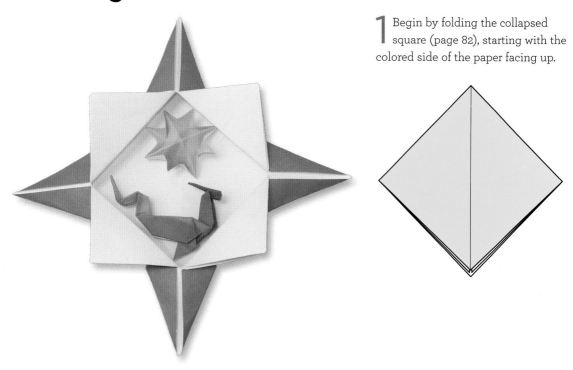

1 Begin by folding the collapsed square (page 82), starting with the colored side of the paper facing up.

2 Fold the crocus (page 86) through Step 9. Fold the corners of the top two layers of paper to their corresponding center fold as shown.

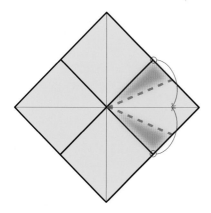

3 Inside reverse fold the folds you made in Step 2.

(continued)

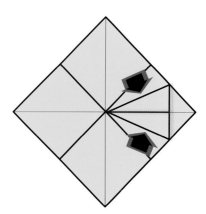

Folding the Ornamental Box continued

4 Your model should look like this. Now perform Steps 2 and 3 on the other three quadrants of your model.

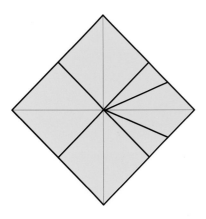

5 Your model should look like this. Fold one of the loose tips in the center to the outside of the square.

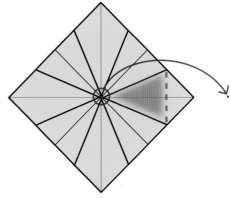

6 Your model should look like this. Repeat Step 5 for the other three tips.

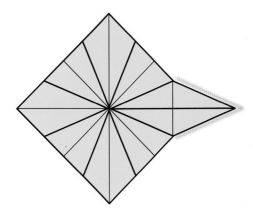

7 Fold the inside corner of the top layers of paper to the outside as shown.

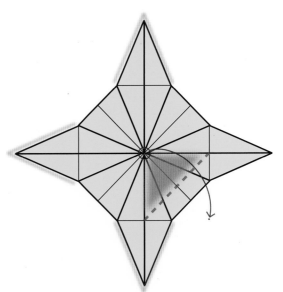

8 Your model should look like this. Repeat Step 7 for the other three quadrants.

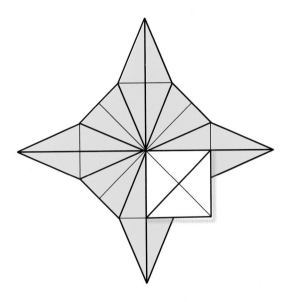

9 Your model should look like this.

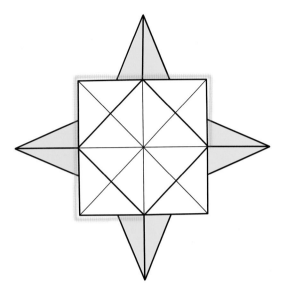

10 Insert your index finger between the bottom layer of paper and each point to shape your box.

Your completed box should look like this.

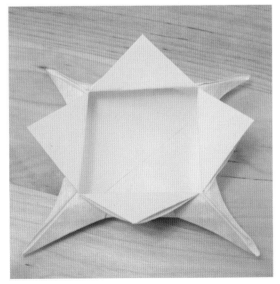

Other Things You Can Do

You can have a lot of fun with this box design. You can draw or color a scene inside a box. I like to glue origami animals inside them.

If you fold your collapsed square starting with the colored side of your paper facing down, the tips will be white and the color will be inside the box.

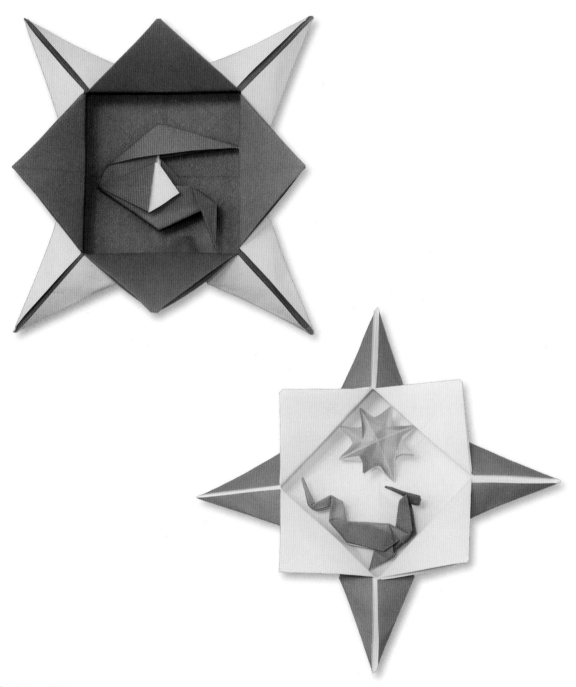

Folding the Tree Ornament

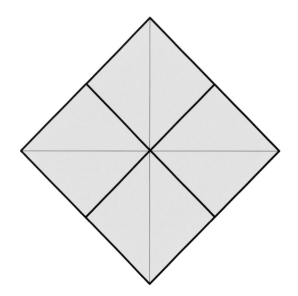

1 Begin by folding the collapsed square (page 82), starting with the colored side of the paper facing up.

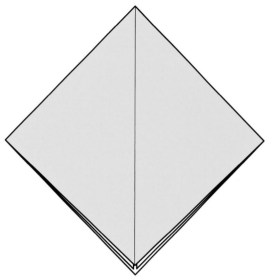

2 Fold the crocus (page 86), through Step 9.

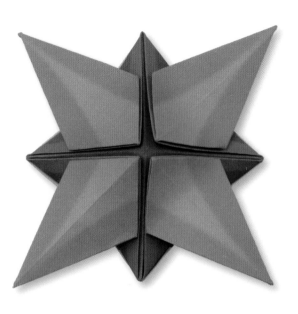

3 Fold the ornamental box (page 99) through Step 5 and then flip your model.

(continued)

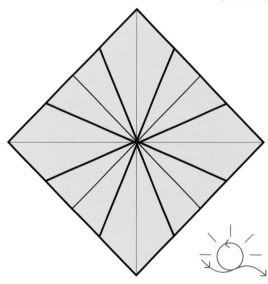

Folding the Tree Ornament continued

4 Fold one corner to the center, but lift your model slightly while doing it to allow the bottom flap to move freely to the outside.

5 Your model should look like this. Repeat Step 4 for the other three corners.

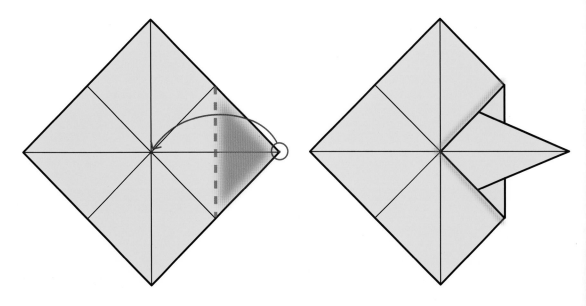

6 Your model should look like this. Flip it.

7 Your model should look like this. Fold one of the center corners to the outside as shown.

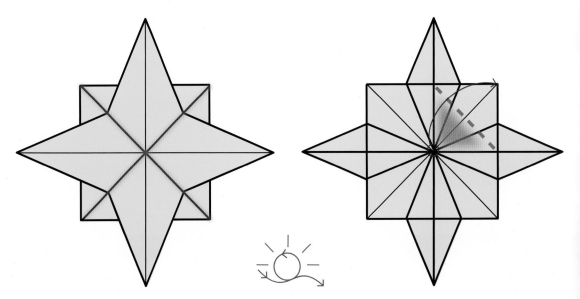

8 Your model should look like this. Repeat Step 7 for the remaining three center corners.

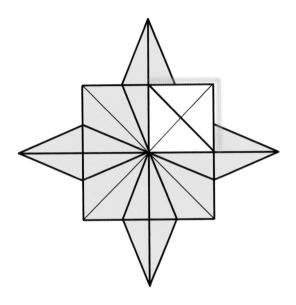

9 Your model should look like this.

10 Insert your index finger into each inner flap while squeezing with the thumb and index finger of your other hand to shape your model. Repeat on the other three corners.

11 Squeeze the four narrow points of your model, pushing them toward the middle to give your ornament a more complex shape.

(continued)

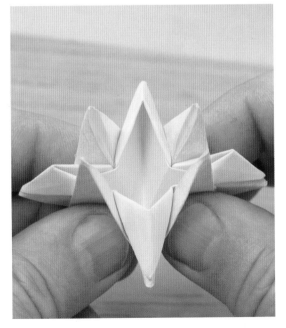

Folding the Tree Ornament continued

12 Your completed tree ornament should look like this.

Other Things You Can Do

You can fold these ornaments starting with the colored side on the inside or on the outside of the collapsed square. When you begin with the color on the outside (as shown in the diagrams on the previous pages), the opposite side of the tree ornament is quite beautiful. Make sure you hang them so they can rotate freely on your tree.

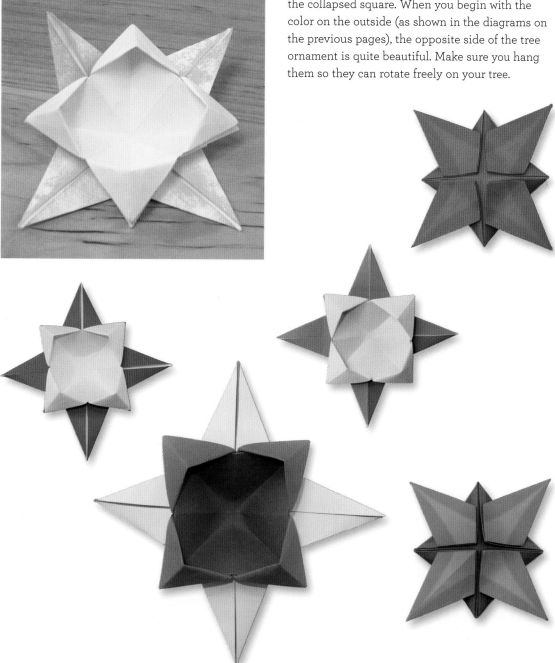

Folding the Flowering Branch

1 Begin by folding the collapsed square (page 82), starting with the colored side of the paper facing up. Fold the left and right corners of the top layer of paper to the center, flip your model, and do the same on the other side.

2A Inside reverse fold all four of the folds you made in Step 1. See the following diagram for help with doing this.

(continued)

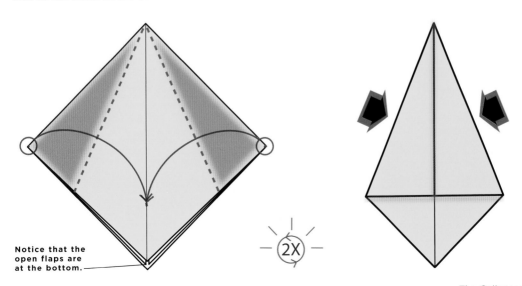

Notice that the open flaps are at the bottom.

2X

Folding the Flowering Branch continued

2B This diagram shows the direction of each fold after Step 2 is completed. Notice that the horizontal, vertical, and long diagonal folds are all valley folds. Notice that the shorter diagonal folds are all mountain folds. If you're having difficulty completing Step 2, unfold your model and, with the colored side facing up, compare the folds to this diagram. Once you're sure each fold is in the proper direction, your square should collapse into a shape that looks just like the next diagram.

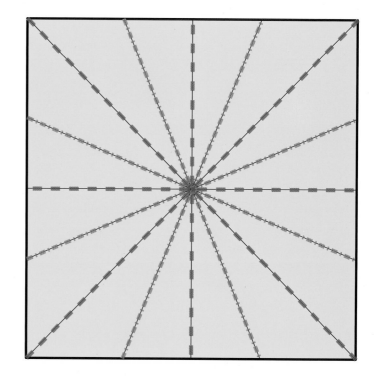

3 Fold the left and right corners of the top layer of paper to the center. Flip your model and repeat on the other side.

4 Inside reverse fold all four flaps you folded in Step 3.

5 Your model should look like this. Book fold your model and repeat Steps 3 and 4 on the other sides.

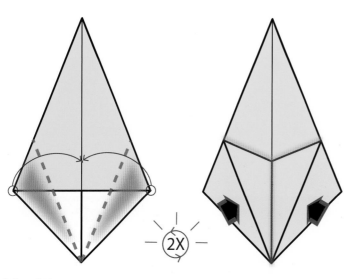

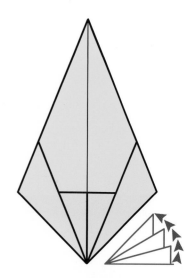

6 Your model should look like this. Fold and then unfold it in half horizontally.

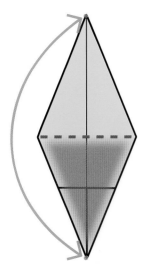

7 Lift the top layer of paper and fold it up on the fold you made in Step 6.

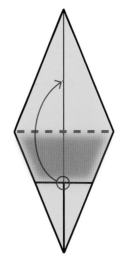

8 Crush fold the flap you created in Step 7 so it lies flat. Flip your model and repeat Steps 7 and 8 on the other side.

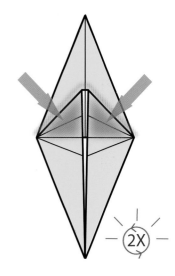

9 Book fold your model and repeat Steps 7 and 8 on the other two sides. Your model will look like this on all four sides.

10 Book fold your model so it looks like this. Make sure there is an even number of layers on both the left and right sides. The underside of your model should look like this as well. The bottom tip has loose flaps under it, the top does not.

11 Fold your model in half vertically.

(continued)

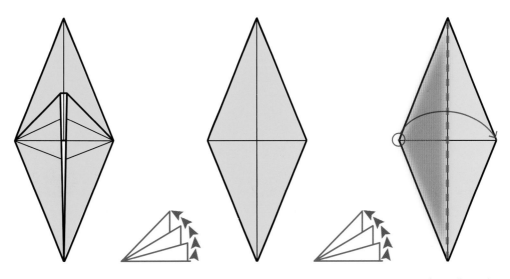

Folding the Flowering Branch continued

12 Fold the top corner down and to the right using the alignment marks as shown. The paper is quite thick here, so just get the fold started in the general direction indicated.

13 Perform an inside reverse fold on the fold you made in Step 12. Make sure you have an even number of layers on each side when you make this fold.

14 Reorient your model and lift it off your work surface. Unfold the top outer layer of paper. This represents one petal.

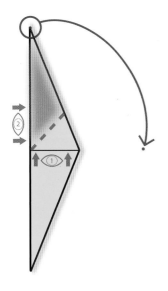

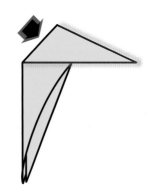

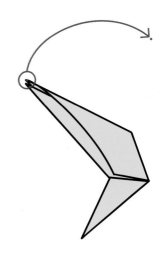

15 Open the other three petals and pinch them at the center to shape the flower.

Your completed flowering branch should look like this.

Other Things You Can Do

This model makes a great lapel pin. You can either tuck the branch portion into an existing buttonhole or use a pin to hold it in place.

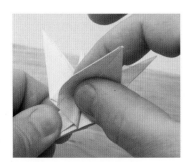

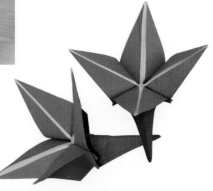

Folding the Fractal Geometric 1

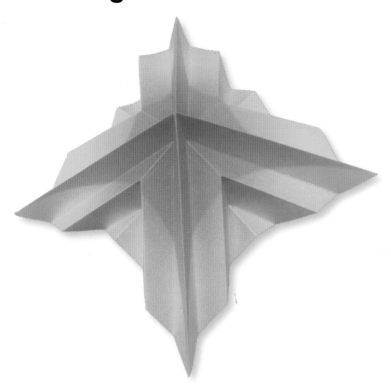

TIP Fold all the layers of paper as shown in the steps that follow. Many of the folds in these diagrams will require reversing; therefore, you should sharpen each fold as you perform it.

1 Begin by folding the collapsed square (page 82), starting with the colored side of the paper facing down. Fold and then unfold each outside corner to the center as shown.

2 Fold and then unfold the left corner to the fold you made in Step 1 on the right side of your model.

(continued)

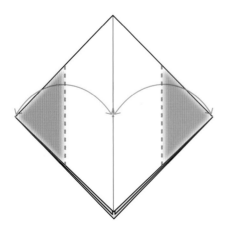

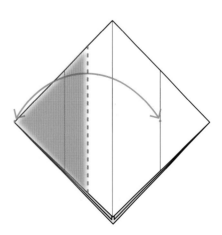

Folding the Fractal Geometric 1 continued

3 Fold and then unfold the right corner to the fold you made in Step 1 on the left side of your model.

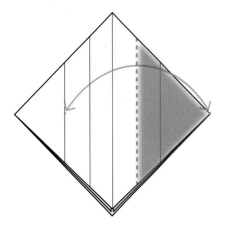

4 Fold and then unfold the outside corners to the folds you made in Step 1 as shown. Completely unfold your model.

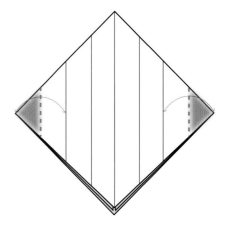

5 Your square should look like this.

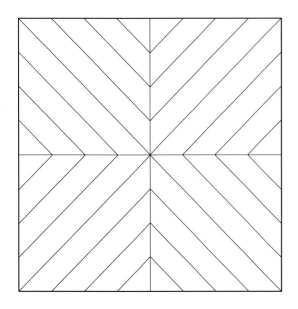

6 You will need to reverse almost half of the folds on your square. Here is a diagram that shows the proper direction of each fold. Notice that the longest diagonal folds don't need to be reversed.

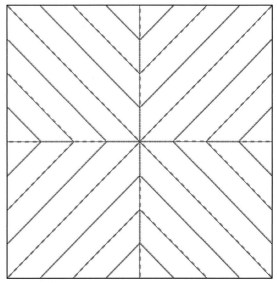

7 Reverse (as necessary) the longest folds (highlighted in blue in this diagram) first. These folds all need to be mountain folds.

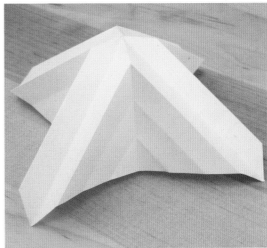

8 Proceed to the second longest folds. These folds all need to be valley folds.

(continued)

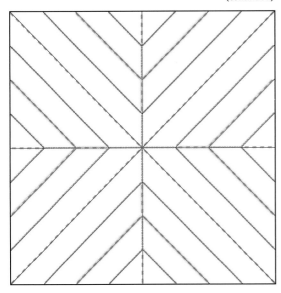

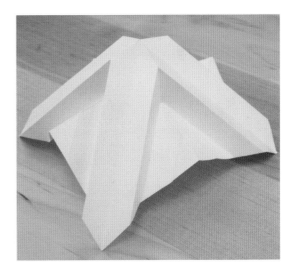

Folding the Fractal Geometric 1 continued

9 Finally, reverse the smallest folds as necessary.

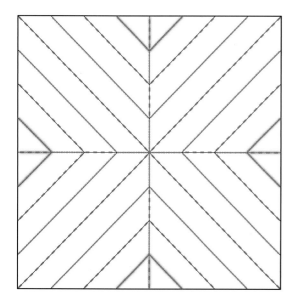

Your completed fractal geometric should look like this.

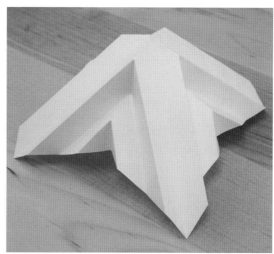

Other Things You Can Do

If you fold each vertical area in half in Step 4, you can double the number of folds making up your fractal shape. You can also turn the shape inside out to form a taller, narrower fractal.

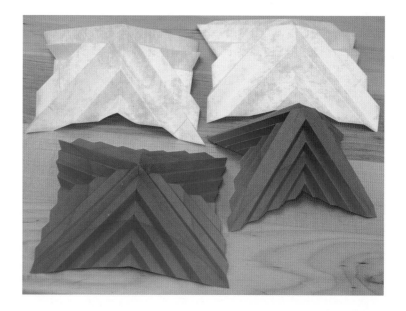

Folding the Pigeon

1 Begin by folding the collapsed square (page 82), starting with the colored side of the paper facing up.

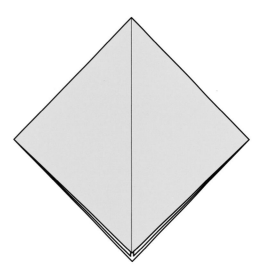

2 Fold the flowering branch (page 107) through Step 8.

3 Fold the top flap down. This is going to represent your pigeon's back. Flip your model.

4 Fold the bottom corner of the top right layers of paper up and to the right, using the inner edge and center horizontal fold for alignment.

(continued)

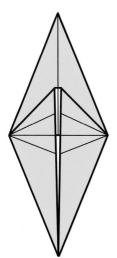

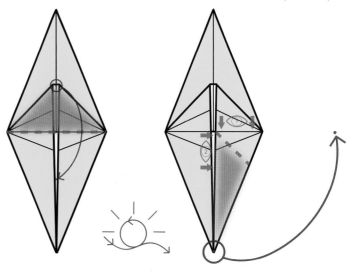

Folding the Pigeon continued

5 Inside reverse fold the fold you made in Step 4. This will form one leg.

6 Repeat Steps 4 and 5 to create a leg on the left side of your model. Your model should look like this. Fold it in half vertically.

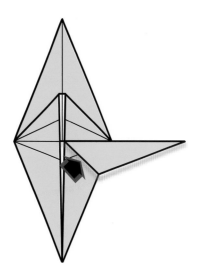

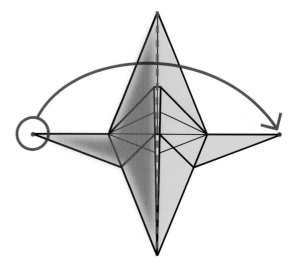

7 Fold the top tip down and to the left. This fold should be well ahead of the thickest layers of paper and almost parallel to the existing fold below.

8 Outside reverse fold the fold you made in Step 7 to form the pigeon's neck.

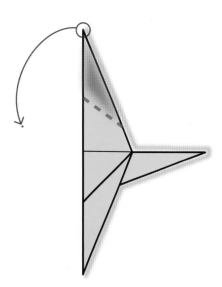

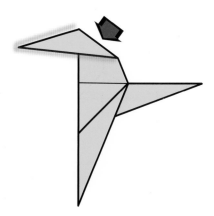

9 Your model should look like this. Fold the left-most tip up and to the right as shown to form the head. The angle of this fold determines whether your bird will be looking up, down, or straight ahead.

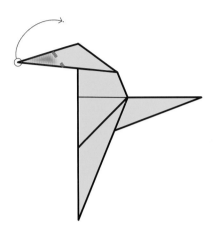

10 Outside reverse fold the fold you made in Step 9.

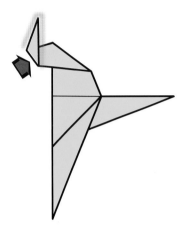

11 Reorient your model. You can add feet to your pigeon by folding each leg's tip up and to the right as shown.

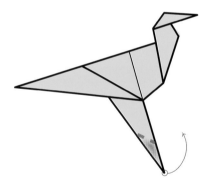

12 Outside reverse fold the folds you made in Step 11 to complete your model.

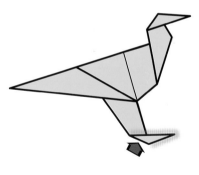

Your completed pigeon should look like this.

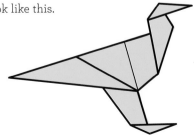

Folding the Scary Bat

1 Begin by folding a collapsed square (page 82), starting with the colored side of the paper facing down.

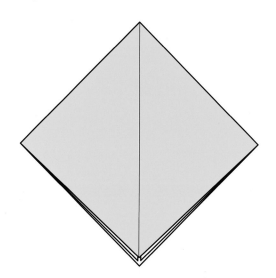

2 Fold the flowering branch (page 107), Steps 1 and 2 completely, and then Steps 3, 4, and 5 on only the top layer of your model. Fold and then unfold your model in half horizontally.

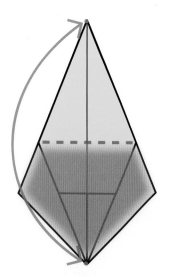

3 Fold the top flap up and…

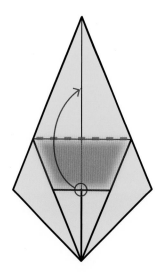

4 …crush fold it so it lies flat.

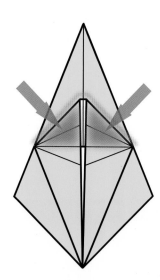

5 Book fold only the top two layers of paper to the left.

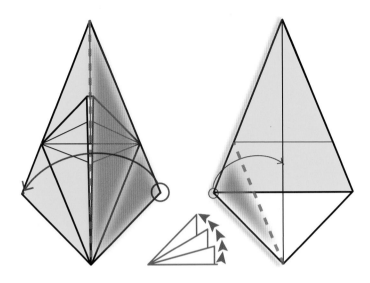

6 Fold the bottom left corner to the center.

7 Inside reverse fold the fold you made in Step 6.

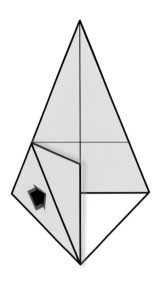

8 Fold the corner of the indicated flap up and to the center fold.

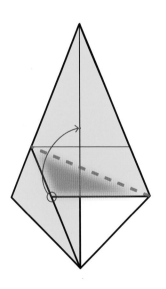

9 Your model should look like this. Book fold the top four layers of paper to the right.

10 Your model should look like this. Fold the bottom right corner up and to the center.

(continued)

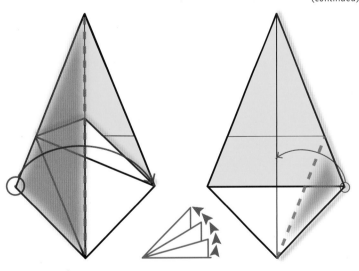

Folding the Scary Bat continued

11 Inside reverse fold the fold you made in Step 10.

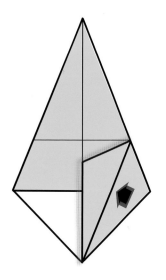

12 Fold the corner of the flap indicated up and to the center fold.

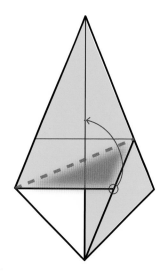

13 Book fold the top two layers of paper to the left.

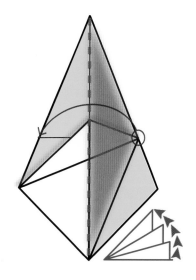

14 Lift your model and pull the lowest layer out on each side.

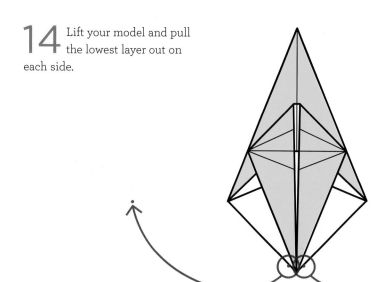

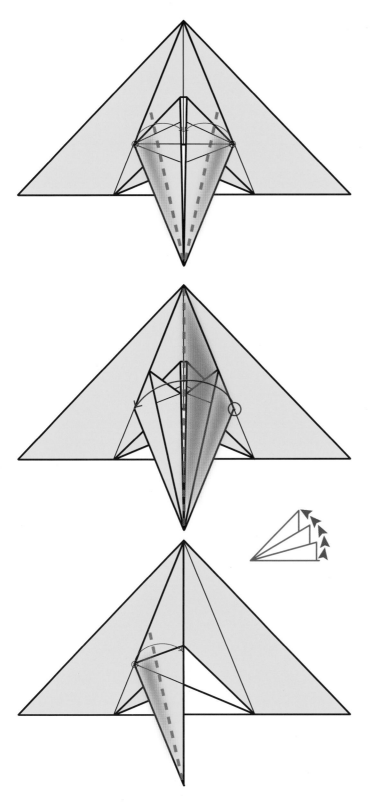

15 Your model should look like this. Now we're going to give our bat some narrow legs. Fold the left and right corners of the top layer to the center.

16 Book fold the top two layers on the inner right to the left.

17 Narrow the flap by folding the left inner corner to the center.

(continued)

Folding the Scary Bat continued

18 Repeat Steps 16 and 17 on the other side to create a second leg. Your model should look like this. Fold the legs up and outward.

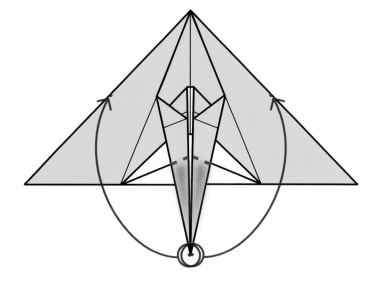

19 Your model should look like this. Inside reverse fold the folds you made in Step 18.

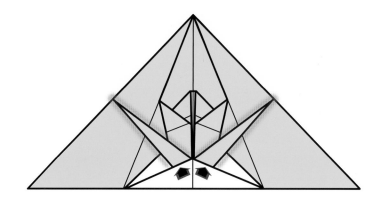

20 Optional: You can fold more complex legs for your bat by making these inside reverse folds on the legs.

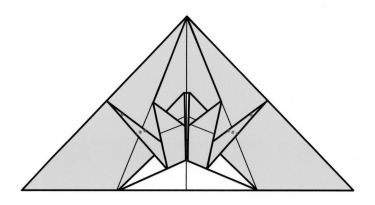

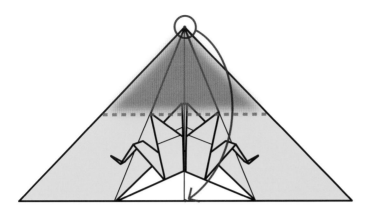

21 Fold your model in half horizontally.

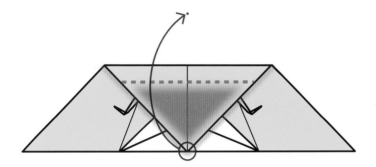

22 Fold the bottom tip you folded in Step 21 back up, leaving a gap.

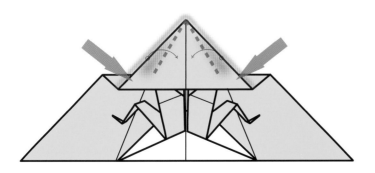

23 Fold the edges of the head to the center as shown. Crush fold the flaps these folds create.

(continued)

Folding the Scary Bat continued

24 Your model should look like this. Flip it.

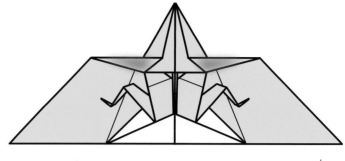

25 Fold your model in half vertically and reorient it so it looks like the next diagram.

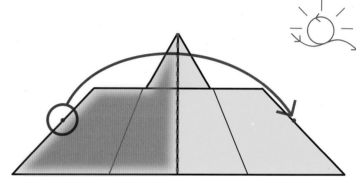

26 Fold the legs of your bat down on both sides of the model.

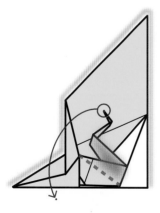

27 Bend the wings down to complete your scary bat.

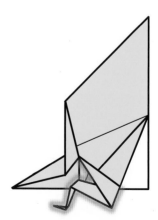

Folding the Lily

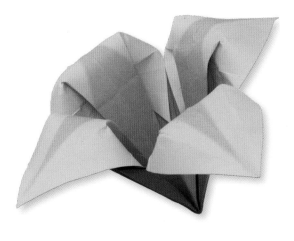

1 Fold the collapsed square (page 82), beginning with the colored side facing down.

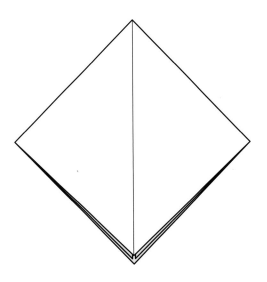

2 Fold the flowering branch (page 107) through Step 9. Pull the flaps out on both sides of your model.

3A Reverse the folds highlighted in blue, open your model a bit, and tuck the flap inside your model. Look at the pictures that follow for clarification.

3B Use your index finger to push the flap to the inside of the model.

(continued)

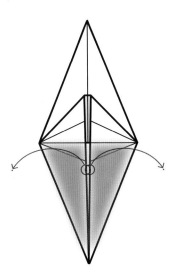

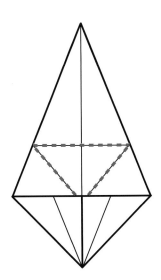

Folding the Lily continued

3C This is what the flap looks like when it's in the right position. Flip your model and tuck the flap in on the opposite side; then book fold and do the other two.

4 After tucking all four flaps into the center of your model, it should look like this.

Book fold one layer on each side of your model.

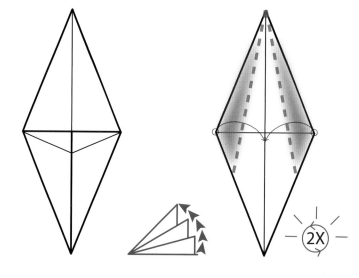

5 With the loose tips at the bottom, fold the upper edges of the top layer of paper toward the center fold. Flip your model and do the same on the other side.

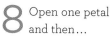

6 Book fold your model and repeat Step 5 on the other two sides. Your model should look like this.

7 Separate the petals at the bottom.

8 Open one petal and then…

9 …push with your index fingers to turn the petal inside out. This will feel unnatural at first, but after you've completed a few flowers, you'll get used to it.

10 Optional: Between each petal you will find a little flap. You can fold this flap up and over the edge if you want to hide any white paper that might show up on the inside of your flower. Your flower will lose a little of its shape if you do this.

Other Things You Can Do

Before making this flower with the yellow paper that comes with this book, I colored the opposite side green.

I glued three blue flowers together and put them in this vase. You can poke a hole in the bottom of a flower and insert a twist-tie. This allows you to attach origami flowers to virtually anything.

The Basic Form

There is little doubt that the basic form revolutionized origami. With its advent, it became possible to make more complex models, including animals with four legs. For those new to origami, folding the basic form can be a challenge. In some respects, it should be approached like a puzzle, but perhaps with the new presentation techniques available in this book it will not seem overwhelming. Many books refer to this shape as the bird base.

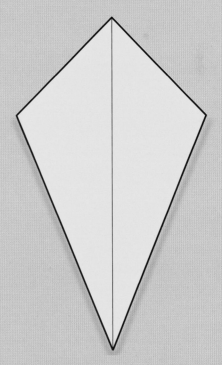

Folding the Basic Form

1 Begin with the collapsed square (page 82).

2 With the open area of the collapsed square at the bottom, fold both the left and right corners of the top pleat of paper to the center.

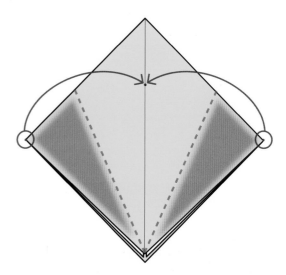

3 Your model should look like this. Flip it.

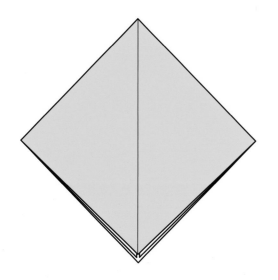

4 Fold the left and right corners to the center just as you did in Step 2.

(continued)

New Symbol: Mountain and Valley Folds—Detailed

Symbol Icon

What makes this confusing is if you flip the paper over, your valley fold suddenly becomes a mountain fold. This causes those new to folding much frustration. Rather than depicting mountain folds, for the most part I will direct you to flip the paper before performing the fold. Occasionally it is necessary to make a true mountain fold. When a mountain fold is required, it will be presented with additional diagrams and/or photographs.

There are two basic types of folds in origami, the mountain fold and the valley fold. The vast majority of folds presented in this book are valley folds. They are both easier to depict and easier to fold. If you put a piece of paper on a flat work surface, fold it in half, and then unfold it, you have performed a valley fold. The way the paper looks after you unfold it is similar to the way a mountain valley looks.

Another problem with mountain folds is that they are hard to show in a diagram. It is easy to create an arrow that shows the folding direction for a valley fold, but a mountain fold requires that the paper be lifted. This is difficult to show with arrows in a two-dimensional diagram. Here is a simple way to create two valley folds and one mountain fold, or if you flip the paper, two mountain folds and one valley fold.

---

1. With the color side up, fold and then unfold the square in half horizontally. Flip your paper.

2. Fold the top edge to the center fold and unfold it, and then fold the bottom edge to the center fold and unfold it.

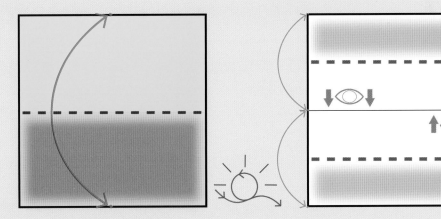

(continued)

New Symbol: Mountain and Valley Folds—Detailed continued

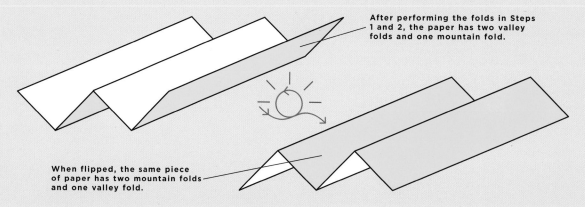

After performing the folds in Steps 1 and 2, the paper has two valley folds and one mountain fold.

When flipped, the same piece of paper has two mountain folds and one valley fold.

Now that you understand the difference between a mountain and a valley fold, I will show you another way that the folds on the previous page might appear in a diagram. When visualizing this set of folding diagrams, think of an accordion.

1. Fold your square in half horizontally.

2. (a) Lift the bottom half of the square and curl the bottom edge under.

   (b) Align the bottom edge (alignment symbol 2) with the fold you made in Step 1 (alignment symbol 1), and then make a crease in the paper. Look at the following pictures to get a better idea of how to perform this fold.

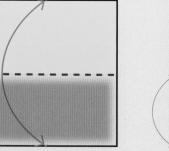

Whenever there is a mountain fold depicted in a diagram, you should carefully read the corresponding instructions.

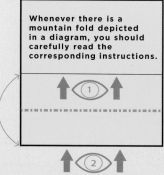

2A.

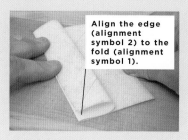

Align the edge (alignment symbol 2) to the fold (alignment symbol 1).

2B.

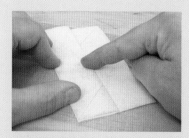

This is a mountain fold.

This is a valley fold.

3. Perform the same fold you did in Step 2 on the other half of the square.

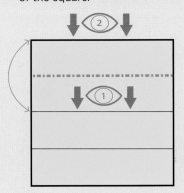

When a diagram calls for a mountain fold, you will see a red line with dots and there will also be a description of how to perform the fold. Glow and afterglow will not be present, as the surfaces they apply to are not visible.

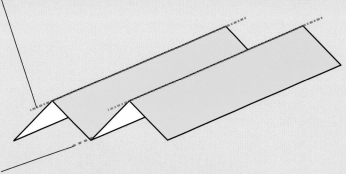

Remember that most folds in this book are valley folds. Valley folds are represented by a dashed green line.

Folding the Basic Form continued

5 Your model should look like this.

The model now has the correct shape; however, the basic form requires that all the loose flaps (there are four of them, two on each side) be moved to the inside. There is a simple method for doing this, explained on the next page.

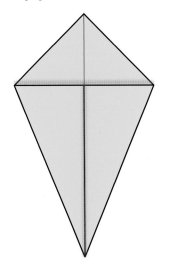

6 When you unfold your model, the folding pattern will look like this. Make sure the colored side of the square is facing up before proceeding to the next step.

(continued)

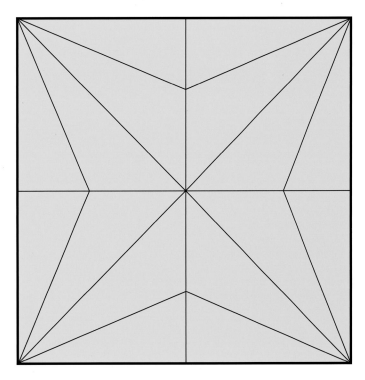

Folding the Basic Form continued

7 This diagram shows the direction of the folds we are interested in as they are now. Reorient your paper so it matches the diagram. In other words, the quarters of your square dominated by mountain folds should be on the lower left and upper right.

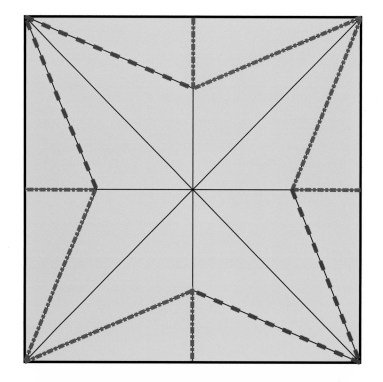

8 Reverse all the folds indicated. It's easy to become confused while you're reversing all these folds. Just remember that all the shorter folds will become valley folds, and that our goal is to tuck the sides inside the shape shown in Step 5.

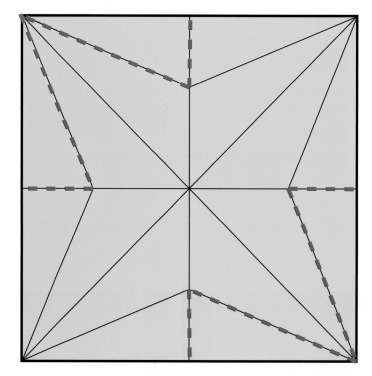

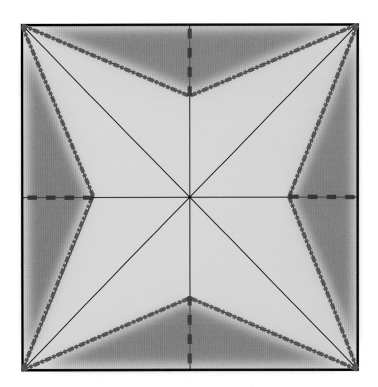

9 Your square should look like this after you have reversed the folds in Step 8. The last step is to collapse the square into the basic form.

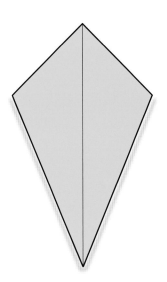

10 Here is the completed basic form model. If your model doesn't look quite as good as this, that's okay. The basic form requires some practice. If your work looks anything like this, you should congratulate yourself!

Folding the Flying Crane

1 Begin with the basic form (page 130). Fold the bottom corner up to the top as shown. Flip your model and repeat this fold on the other side.

2 Book fold both sides of your model.

(continued)

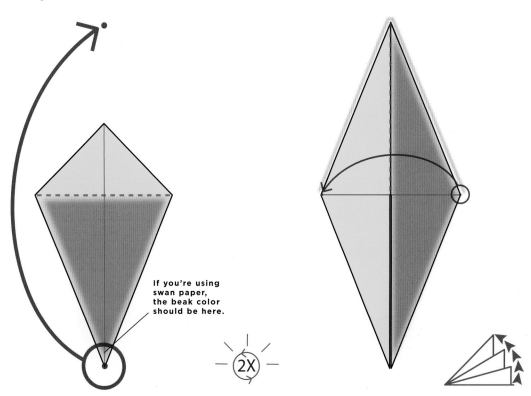

If you're using swan paper, the beak color should be here.

2X

New Symbol: Pull and Pinch

Symbol Icon

The pull and pinch technique is an easy-to-master sequence of movements. Typically, a folded model's appendage is pulled out from its original position, and then the resultant pockets that form at the other end of it are pinched into place. This technique can also be used to adjust the angle of heads, legs, and feet, allowing you to fine-tune poses and adjust models so they will stand on their own.

1. Here is an example of the pull and pinch technique. The left-hand narrow tip will be pulled down, creating a pocket at the pink arrows. This pocket is pinched to secure the tip in its new position.

2. As you pull the narrow tip down, two pockets form at its base (only one is visible, just below my left thumb in the picture).

3. Pinch these pockets to secure the narrow tip in place.

Folding the Flying Crane continued

3 Fold the bottom corner of the top layer up and to the right, as shown, on both sides of your model.

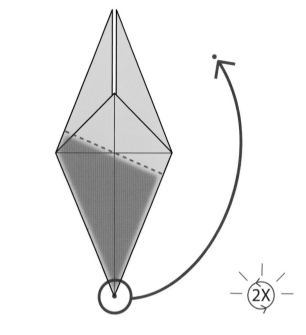

4 Pull the tips out and down, as shown, and then pinch as indicated to secure them. Notice that the upper edge of the left tip (in the next diagram) aligns with the fold line visible toward the bottom of the model.

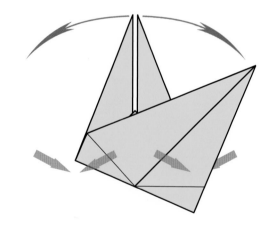

5 Your model should look like this. Fold the left corner down to form the head.

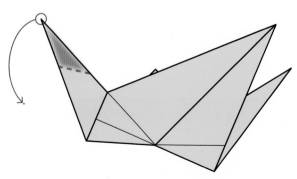

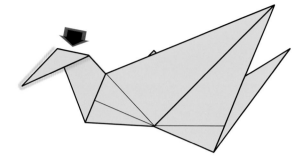

6 Inside reverse fold the fold you made in Step 5.

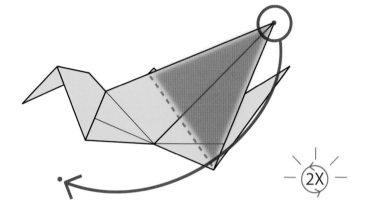

7 Fold the wings down on both sides of your model. This fold line should be roughly perpendicular to the upper edge of the tail.

2X

Other Things You Can Do

Pinch the front lower corner and pull the tail, and your bird will flap its wings.

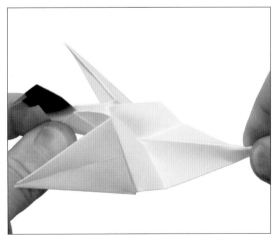

Folding the Sitting Crane

1 Begin with the basic form (page 130). Fold the bottom corner up to the top as shown. Flip your model and repeat this fold on the other side.

2 Fold the left and right corners of the top layer to the center. Flip your model and repeat on the opposite side.

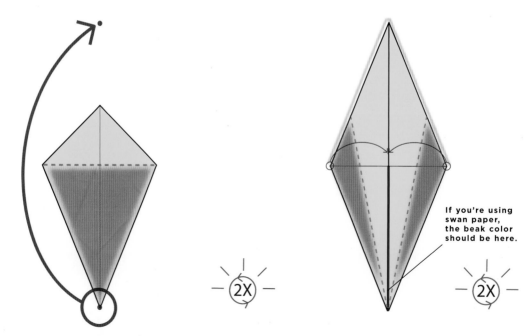

If you're using swan paper, the beak color should be here.

2X

2X

3 Book fold one layer on each side of your model.

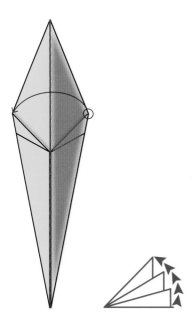

4 Fold the bottom corner of the upper layer to the top of your model. Flip it and repeat the fold on the other side.

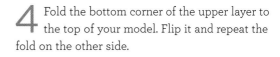

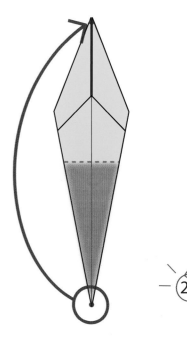

5 Your model should look like this. Book fold one layer on each side.

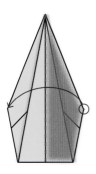

6 Fold the top corner of the upper layer down, and then flip your model and do the same on the other side.

(continued)

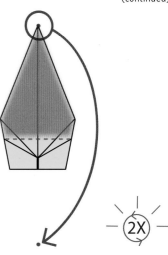

Folding the Sitting Crane *continued*

7 Pull the left narrow tip down and toward the left, and then pinch in the area indicated to secure it. Do the same with the tip on the right.

8 Fold one of the tips down, as shown, to form the head.

9 Inside reverse fold the fold you made in Step 8.

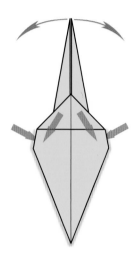

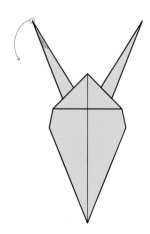

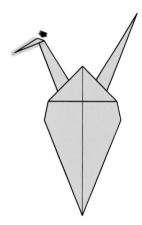

10 Lift the wings up a bit on both sides.

Your completed sitting crane should look like this.

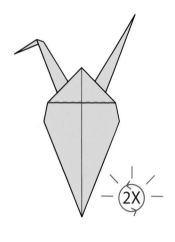

Folding the Old Crow

1 Begin with the basic form (page 130). Fold the bottom corner up to the top as shown. Flip your model and repeat this fold on the other side.

2 Fold the left bottom tip up and to the left.

(continued)

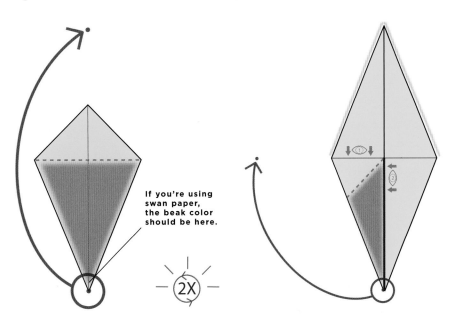

If you're using swan paper, the beak color should be here.

2X

Folding the Old Crow continued

3 Inside reverse fold the fold you made in Step 2.

4 Repeat Steps 2 and 3 on the right side of your model. Your model will look like this. Fold the top corner of the upper layer down to the bottom on the pre-existing fold.

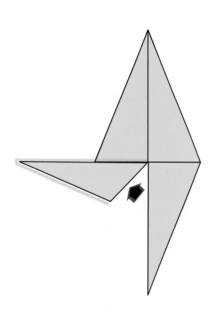

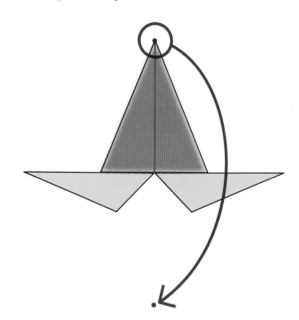

5 Your model should look like this. Flip it.

6 Fold your model in half vertically.

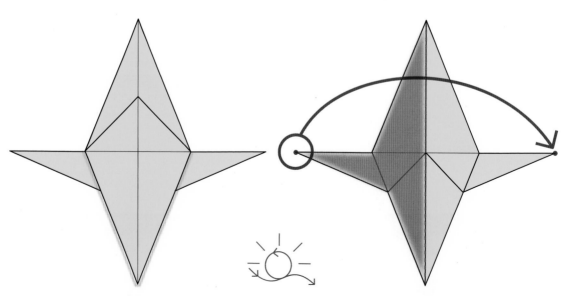

7 Your model should look like this. Fold the top corner down and to the right to form the head.

8 Inside reverse fold the fold you made in Step 7.

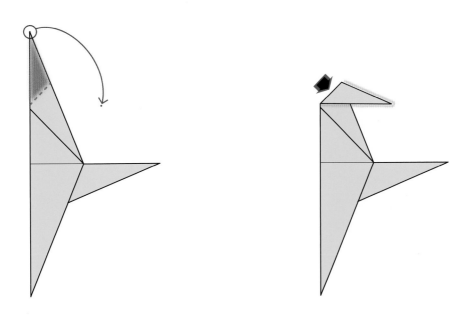

Your completed old crow should look like this.

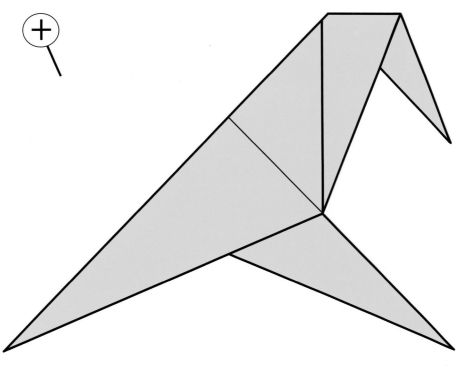

Folding the Sea Lion

1 Begin by folding the basic form (page 130).

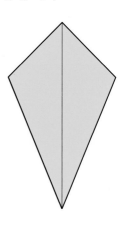

2 Fold the old crow (page 143) through Step 5. Fold the right tip up and to the left using the edges as shown for alignment.

3 Outside reverse fold the fold you made in Step 2.

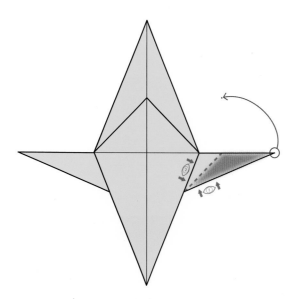

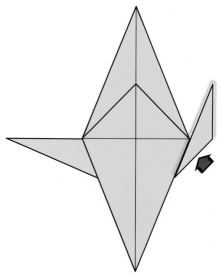

4 Repeat Steps 2 and 3 on the left tip, and your model should look like this. Fold the upper right tip down and to the right as shown.

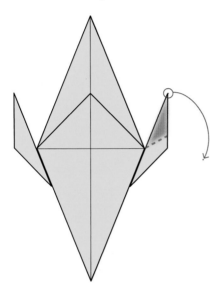

5 Outside reverse fold the fold you made in Step 4.

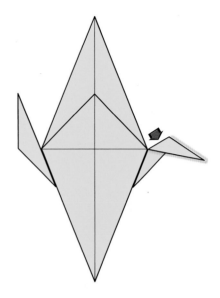

6 Repeat Steps 4 and 5 on the left tip, and your model should look like this. Fold it in half vertically.

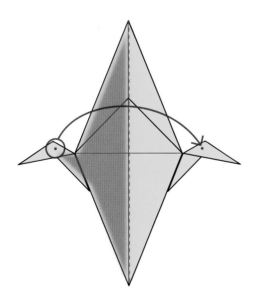

7 Fold the top tip down and to the left, using the edge and horizontal fold, as shown, for alignment. This fold will encompass all the layers beneath it, so it will be a bit of a challenge on your first attempt.

(continued)

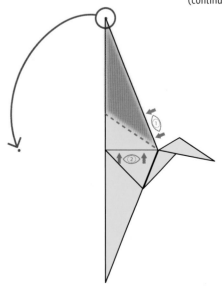

Folding the Sea Lion continued

8 Outside reverse fold the fold you made in Step 7. Look at the next diagram for clarification.

9 Fold the bottom tip up and to the right to form the body of the sea lion. This fold is roughly parallel to the paper edge above it, but the distance from that edge is up to you. Fold it farther from the edge to create a larger body, closer to create a smaller one.

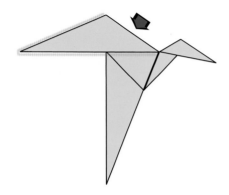

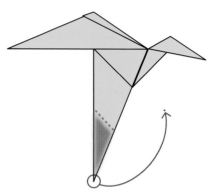

10 Inside reverse fold the fold you made in Step 9.

11 Fold all the layers up and to the left, as shown, to form a rear flipper.

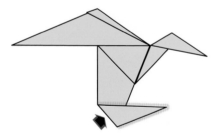

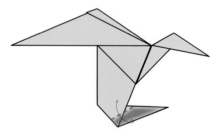

12 Outside reverse fold the fold you made in Step 11. Reorient your model so it looks like the next diagram.

13 Fold the top tip to the right as shown.

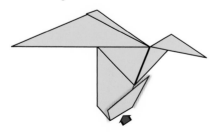

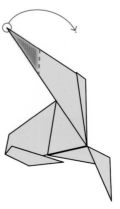

14 Outside reverse fold the fold you made in Step 13.

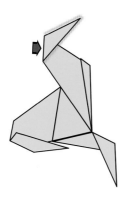

15 Tuck the tip of the nose underneath to form a head shape similar to a seal.

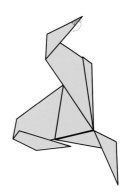

Your completed sea lion should look like this. You can spread its front flippers to obtain a more natural look.

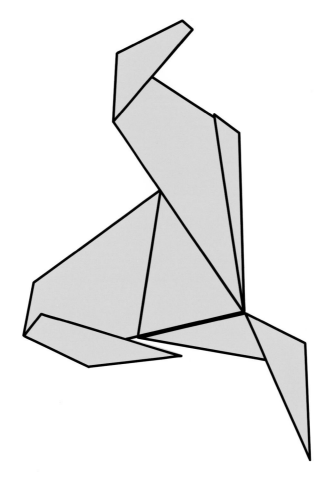

Folding the Silly Goose

1 Begin by folding the basic form (page 130).

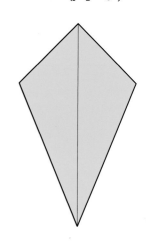

2 Fold the old crow (page 143) through Step 5.

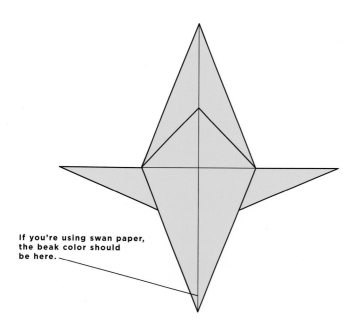

If you're using swan paper, the beak color should be here.

3 Fold the sea lion (page 146) through Step 3. Fold the bottom tip up to the top on the pre-existing fold.

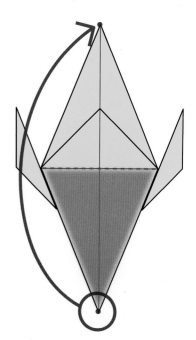

4 Fold the bottom corner of the top layer up, as shown, on the left and right sides of your model. Flip your model and do the same on the other side.

5 Your model should look like this. Fold and then unfold the outer tips down and toward the center as shown.

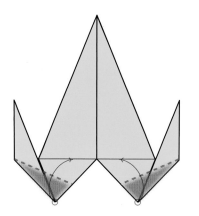

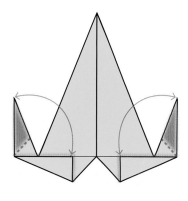

6 Now fold and then unfold the tips toward the center of the model, using the folds you made in Step 5 and the outside edge of the paper for alignment.

7 T-fold the folds you made in Steps 5 and 6.

(continued)

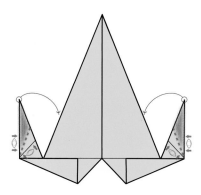

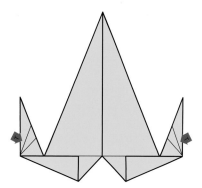

Folding the Silly Goose continued

8 Fold the top corner of the upper layer down as shown.

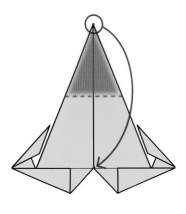

9 Fold the edge created by the fold you made in Step 8 down on the existing fold at the bottom of your model.

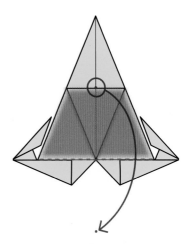

10 Your model should look like this. Flip it.

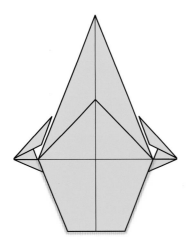

11 Fold your model in half vertically.

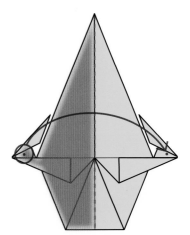

12
Fold the bottom left corner up and to the right as shown.

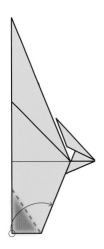

13
Inside reverse fold the fold you made in Step 12.

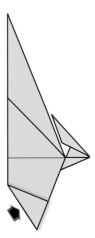

14
Align the right outside edge (alignment symbol 1) with the model's inner edge (alignment symbol 2). Fold and then unfold.

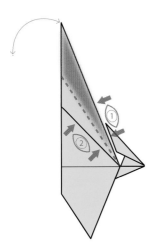

15
Fold the top corner down and to the left, using the horizontal center fold for alignment.

(continued)

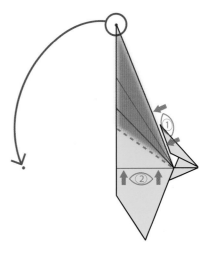

Folding the Silly Goose continued

16 Outside reverse fold the fold you made in Step 15.

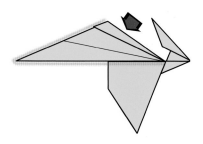

17 Outside reverse fold the fold you made in Step 14. Reorient your model so it matches the next diagram.

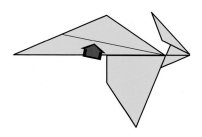

18 Fold and then unfold the upper tip down as shown.

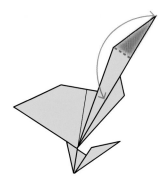

19 Fold and then unfold the upper tip down as shown.

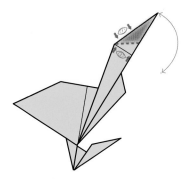

20 T-fold the folds you made in Steps 18 and 19.

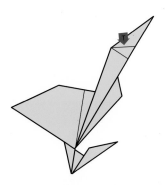

21 Your model should look like this. Pull the T-folds you made in Step 7 down to form the goose's feet.

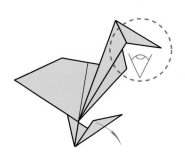

22 Open the T-fold you made in Step 20 and make these folds to form the goose's bill.

Your completed silly goose should look like this.

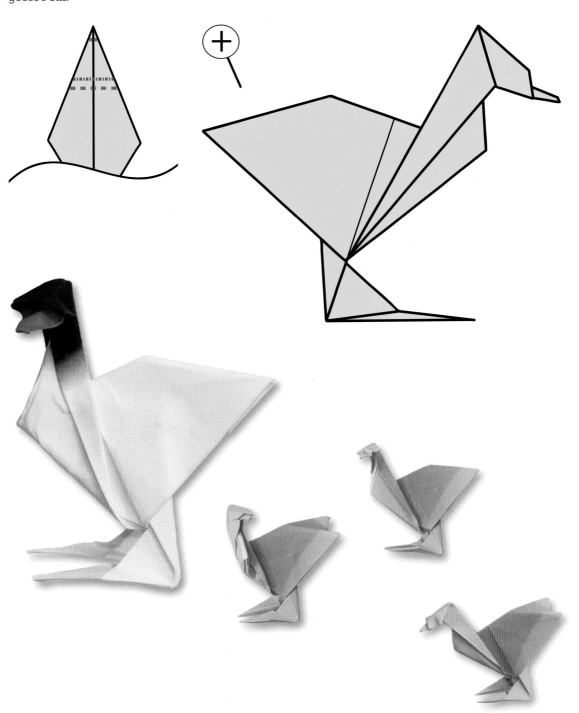

Folding the Rooster

1 Begin by folding the basic form (page 130).

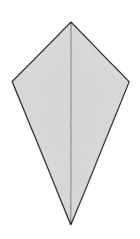

2 Fold the old crow (page 143) through Step 5.

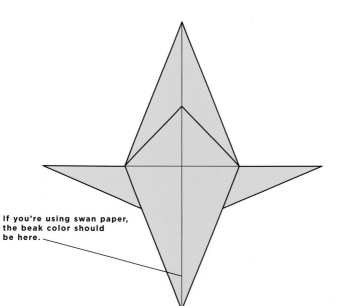

If you're using swan paper, the beak color should be here.

3 Fold the sea lion (page 146) through Step 3. Fold the outer tips down and toward the center of the model.

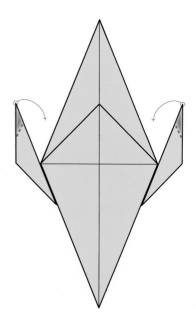

4 Inside reverse fold the folds you made in Step 3.

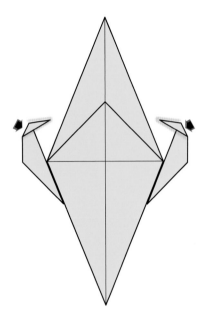

5 Your model should look like this. Fold it in half vertically.

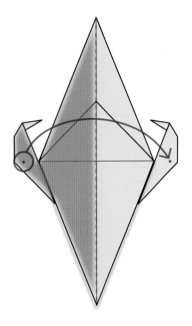

6 Fold the top tip down and to the left, using the outer edge and existing fold line to align it.

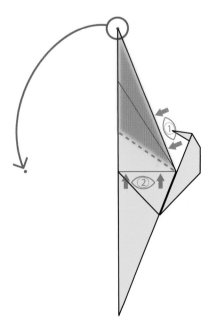

7 Outside reverse fold the fold you made in Step 8.

(continued)

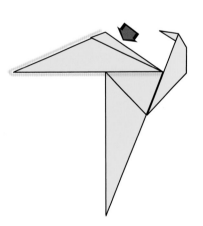

Folding the Rooster continued

8 Fold and then unfold the bottom corner up to the top as shown.

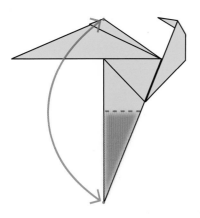

9 Fold and then unfold the bottom corner up and to the left as shown.

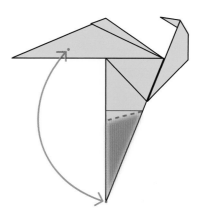

10 Outside reverse fold the fold you made in Step 8. The bottom tip will end up inside the top area created in Step 9.

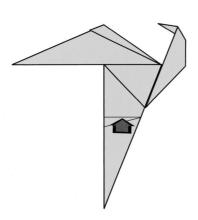

11 Outside reverse fold the fold you made in Step 9. Reorient your model so it looks like the next diagram. If you have trouble completing this fold, try doing Steps 10 and 11 at the same time.

12 Fold the right tip down and to the right to form the rooster's head.

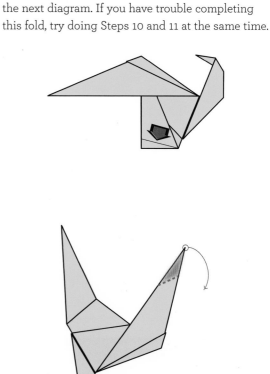

13 Outside reverse fold the fold you made in Step 12.

14 To create a beak, fold the tip of the head back (underneath) and then forward again, leaving a small gap.

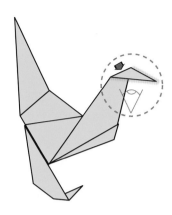

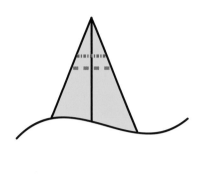

Your completed rooster should look like this. You can curl your rooster's tail if you so desire. The rooster doesn't have much surface area on his feet, so making him stand on his own can be a challenge. One solution is to flatten the feet or make them larger in Step 3 (perform the folds a bit lower).

Folding the Flamingo

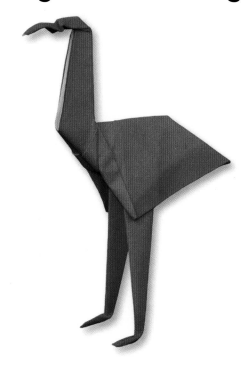

1 Begin by folding the basic form (page 130).

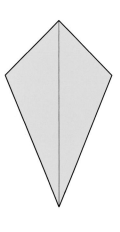

2 Fold the old crow (page 143) through Step 5 and then flip it.

3 Fold the left and right edges of the top layer as shown. Notice that the fold lines don't extend all the way to the bottom corner of the areas. Small pockets form at the bottom of each fold which you…

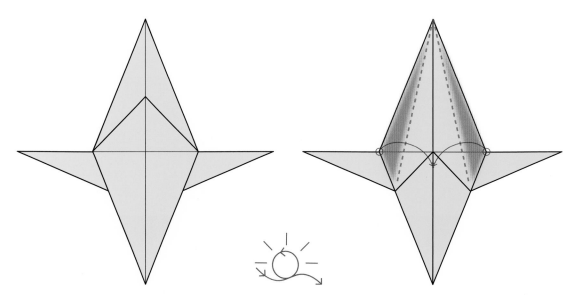

4 ...crush fold into place.

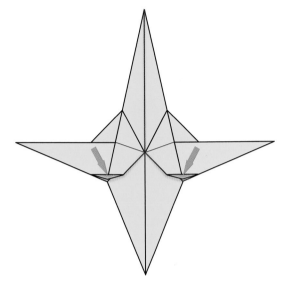

5 Fold the top layer of the left side up as shown.

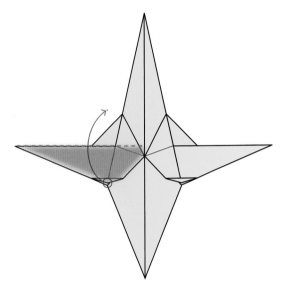

6 Fold the top and bottom edges of the left side to the center as shown. This will create a narrow leg.

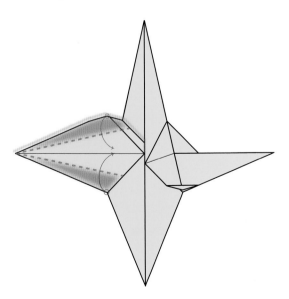

7 Close the flap you opened in Step 5.

(continued)

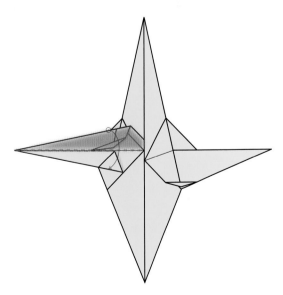

Folding the Flamingo continued

8 Repeat Steps 5, 6, and 7 on the right side of your model. Your model should then look like this. Fold the bottom tip up and toward the center as shown.

9 Fold your model in half vertically.

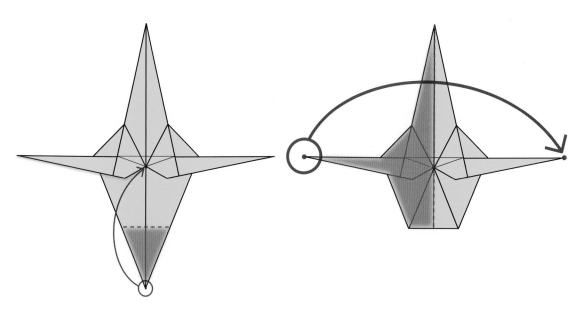

10 Fold the bottom left corner up and to the right as shown.

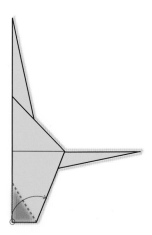

11 Inside reverse fold the fold you made in Step 10.

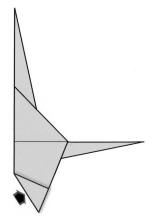

12 Fold all layers down and toward the left, as shown, using the upper edge and the fold line for alignment.

13 Outside reverse fold the fold you made in Step 12. Reorient your model so it looks like the next diagram.

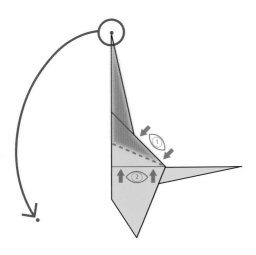

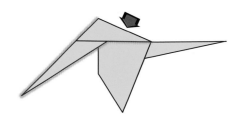

14 Fold the top tip down and to the right to form the head.

15 Outside reverse fold the fold you made in Step 14.

16 Make a mountain and valley fold to create the flamingo's head, leaving as much room as possible for the beak.

(continued)

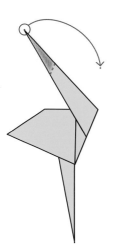

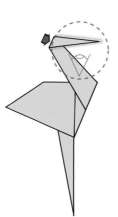

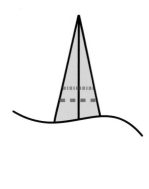

Folding the Flamingo continued

17 Fold the bottom tip up and to the right, as shown, on both sides of your model.

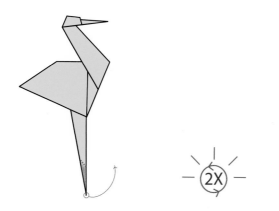

18 Outside reverse fold the folds you made in Step 17.

19 Your completed flamingo should look like this. You can curve the beak by pinching it. Flattening the feet will make it easier for your model to stand on its own.

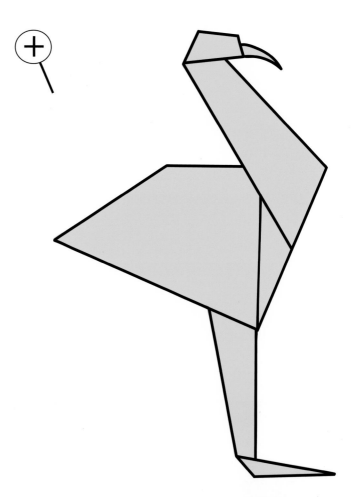

Folding the Mosquito

1 Begin by folding the basic form (page 130).

2 Fold the old crow (page 143) through Step 5.

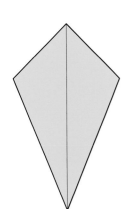

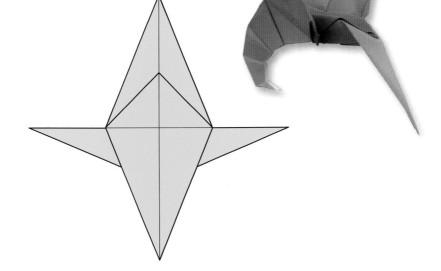

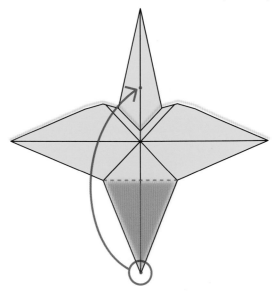

3 Fold the flamingo (page 160) through Step 4. Open the left and right flaps as shown.

4 Fold the bottom tip up as shown.

(continued)

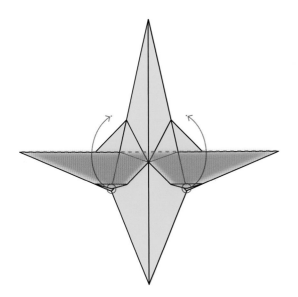

Folding the Mosquito continued

5 Fold the flap back down, leaving a small gap.

6 Your model should look like this. Fold the bottom tip up again, leaving a gap about four times the size of the gap you left in Step 5; then fold it back down, leaving a gap similar to the one you left in Step 5. Repeat these folds on the flap until you run out of space.

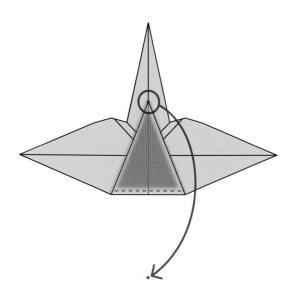

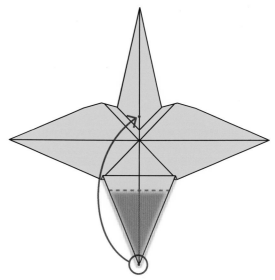

7 Your model should look similar to this. Flip it.

8 Fold the outer corners of the top flap down and toward the center of the model as shown.

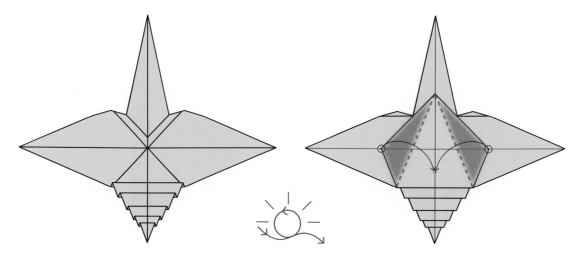

9 Fold your model in half vertically and reorient it so it looks like the following diagram.

10 Pull each pleat down and to the right, and then pinch it to secure it in position. See the next diagram for a clearer explanation.

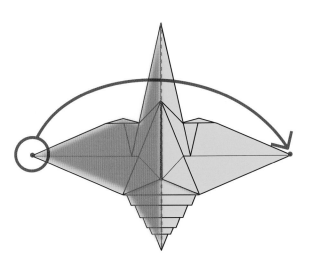

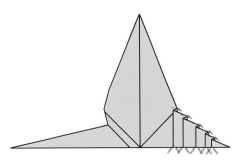

11 Fold the left tip down and to the right. This fold is made just ahead of the thickest layers of paper, so you can feel where it belongs.

12 Outside reverse fold the fold you made in Step 11.

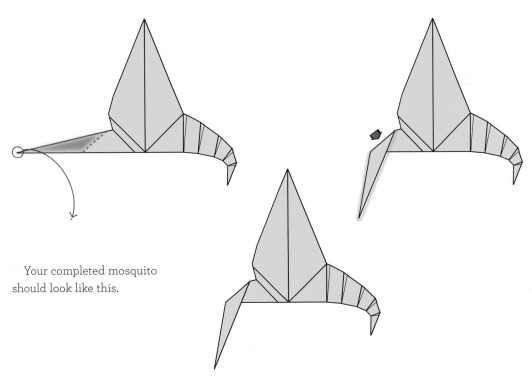

Your completed mosquito should look like this.

Folding the Sea Gull

1 Begin by folding the basic form (page 130).

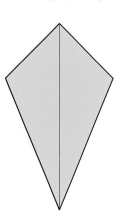

2 Fold the old crow (page 143) through Step 5. Fold the outside tips up and toward the center as shown.

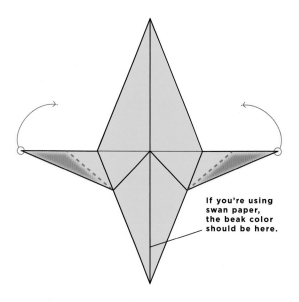

If you're using swan paper, the beak color should be here.

3 Outside reverse fold the folds you made in Step 2.

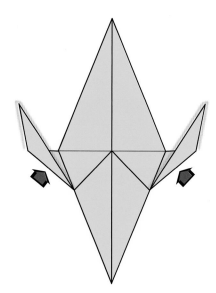

4 Fold the top two layers of paper up (on the existing fold), as shown, on both the left and right sides of your model. Allow the tips you folded in Step 2 to rotate freely.

5 Your model should look like this. Fold it in half vertically.

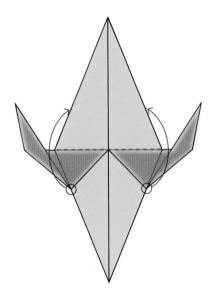

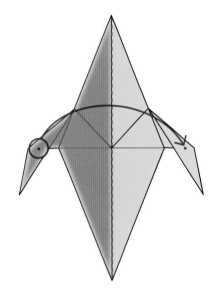

6 Fold and then unfold the bottom corner up and to the left.

7 Fold the bottom corner up and to the left as shown.

(continued)

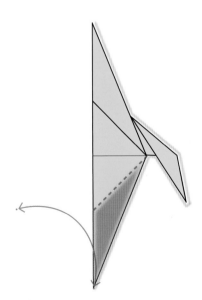

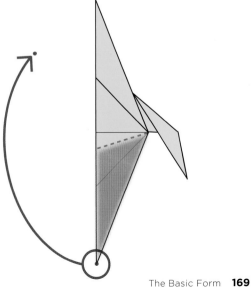

Folding the Sea Gull *continued*

8 Outside reverse fold the fold you made in Step 7.

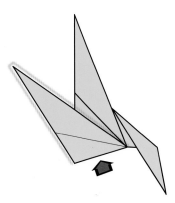

9 Outside reverse fold the fold you made in Step 6.

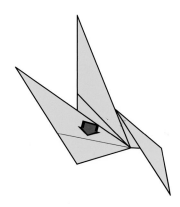

10 Fold and then unfold the left tip to the right. Use the bottom edge for alignment.

11 Fold and then unfold the left tip down, using the top edge and the fold you made in Step 10 for alignment.

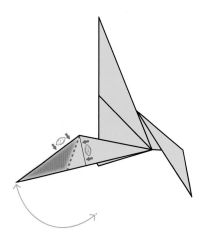

12
T-fold the folds you made in Steps 10 and 11.

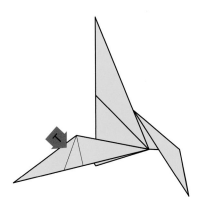

13
Your model should look like this. Open the T-fold and…

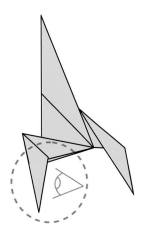

14
…fold a valley and mountain fold to create a beak. Close the T-fold.

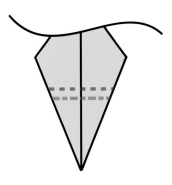

15
Reorient your model so it looks like this. Fold and then unfold both the bottom tips up.

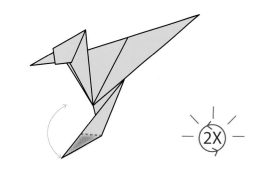

16
Open the bottom tips and pinch the folds you made in Step 15 to form what look like webbed feet. Your completed sea gull should look like this.

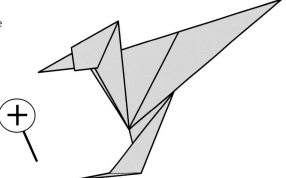

Folding the Flying Dragon

1 Begin by folding the basic form (page 130).

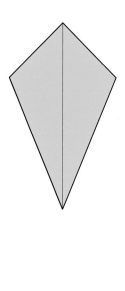

2 Fold the old crow (page 143) through Step 4.

3 Fold the flamingo (page 160) through Step 5 and then flip it.

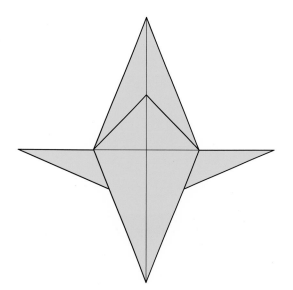

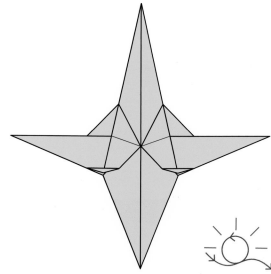

4 Fold the top layer of the bottom tip up to the top.

5 Narrow the top tips by folding the edges to the center as shown. Notice that the fold line does not extend all the way to the bottom edge of your paper. This is because you will have to...

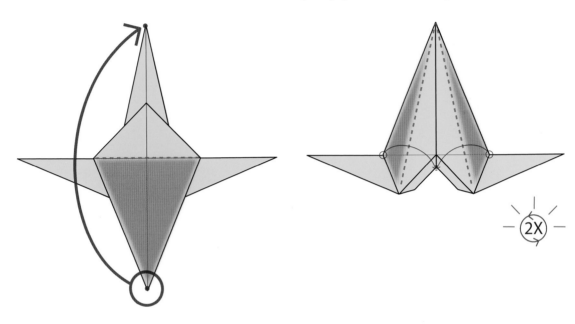

6 ...crush fold the flaps at the bottom.

7 Fold the top layer of paper down as shown.

(continued)

Folding the Flying Dragon continued

8 Fold the small flap down and then flip your model.

9 Fold the top layer of paper up on both the left and right sides of your model.

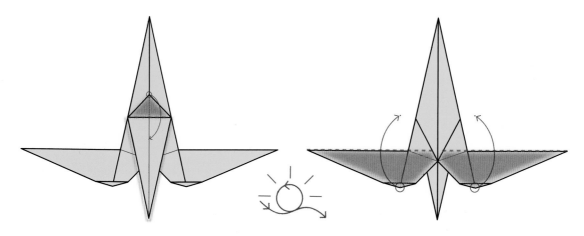

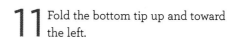

10 Fold your model in half vertically.

11 Fold the bottom tip up and toward the left.

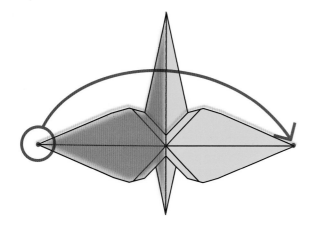

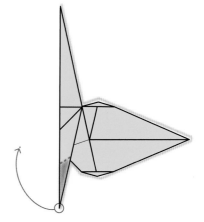

12 Outside reverse fold the fold you made in Step 11.

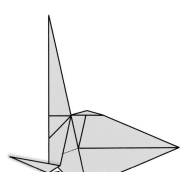

13 Fold the narrow tip to the right and slightly down.

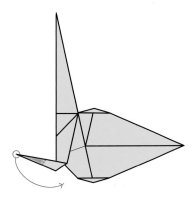

14 Outside reverse fold the fold you made in Step 13.

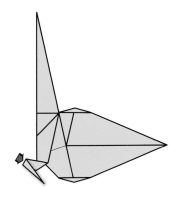

15 Pull the flap you folded in Step 8 toward the outside of the model, and then pinch in the area shown to secure it.

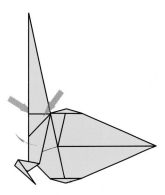

Your completed flying dragon should look like this.

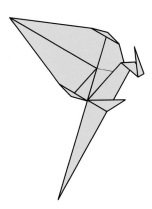

Folding the Tyrannosaurus Rex

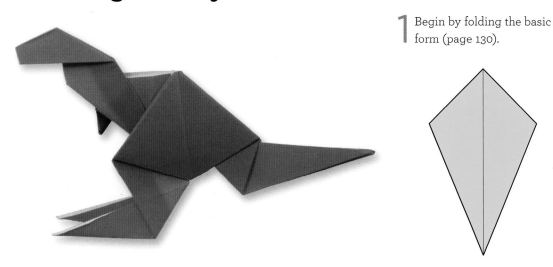

1 Begin by folding the basic form (page 130).

2 Fold the old crow (page 143) through Step 4. Fold the outside tips down and toward the center.

3 Inside reverse fold the folds you made in Step 2.

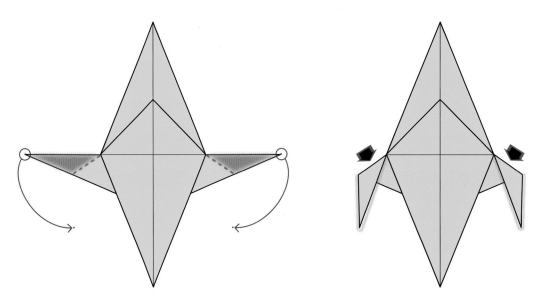

4 Fold your model in half vertically.

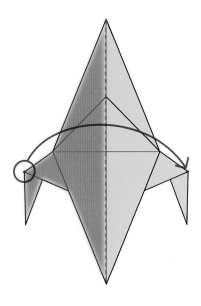

5 Fold the top tip down and to the left. This fold is made just ahead of the thickest area of paper, so you can feel where the fold line should be.

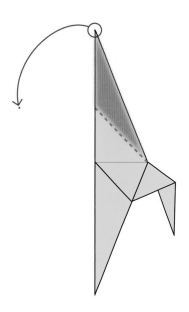

6 Outside reverse fold the fold you made in Step 5.

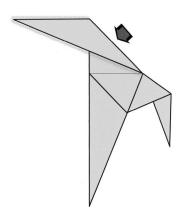

7 Fold the top two layers of paper up on the existing fold on both sides of your model.

(continued)

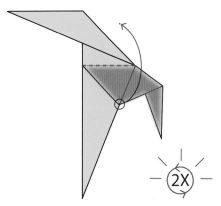

2X

Folding the Tyrannosaurus Rex continued

8 Fold and then unfold the bottom tip up and to the right, aligning the left edge to the fold as shown.

9 Fold and then unfold the bottom corner again, parallel to the fold you made in Step 8 but a bit farther down.

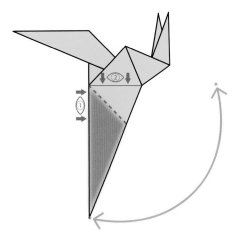

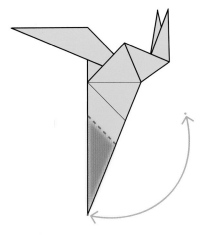

10 Inside reverse fold the fold you made in Step 8.

11 Inside reverse fold the fold you made in Step 9.

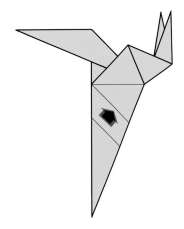

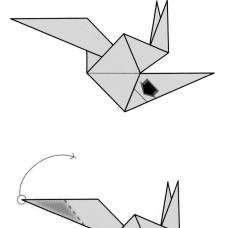

12 Your model should look like this. Fold the left tip up and to the right to form the head of the dinosaur.

13 Outside reverse fold the fold you made in Step 12, and then reorient your model so it looks like the next diagram.

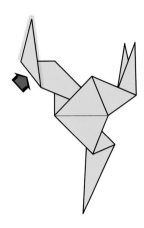

14 Fold the tip of the head underneath to form a nose and then pull the flap inside the neck down, pinch it, then pull it back up to form a tiny appendage.

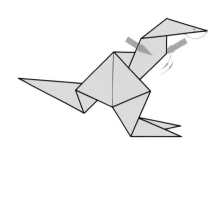

Your completed tyrannosaurus rex should look like this.

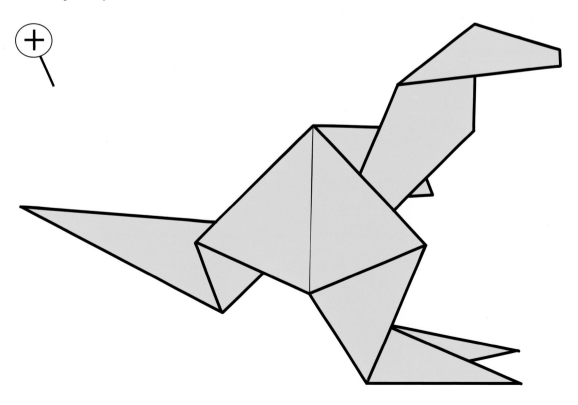

The Collapsed Triangle

The collapsed triangle is similar to the collapsed square except that we begin with the colored side of the paper facing down.

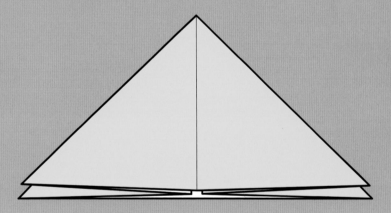

Folding the Collapsed Triangle

1 Begin with the colored side of the paper facing down.

2 Fold and then unfold your square in half diagonally.

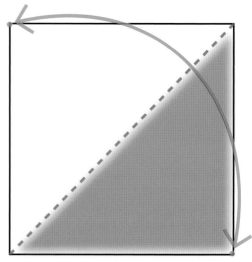

3 Fold and then unfold your square in half on the other diagonal and then flip your paper.

4 Fold and then unfold your square in half horizontally.

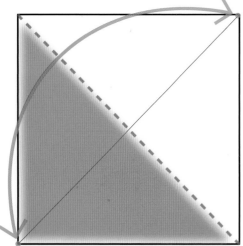

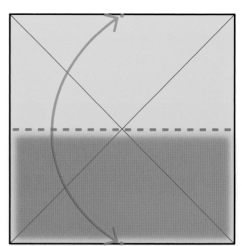

5 Fold and then unfold your
square vertically.

6 Your paper should look like this. Notice that
the diagonals are mountain folds and the
horizontal and vertical are valley folds. Pinch the
mountain folds to collapse it into a triangle (just as
you did on the collapsed square).

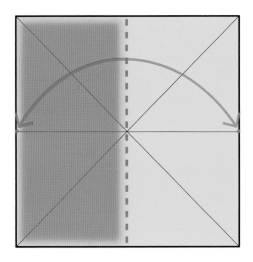

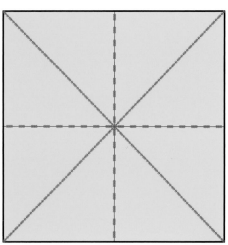

Your completed collapsed triangle should look like this.

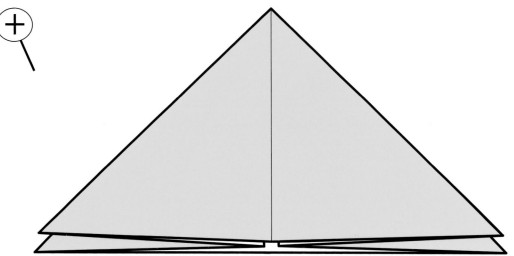

Folding the Frog

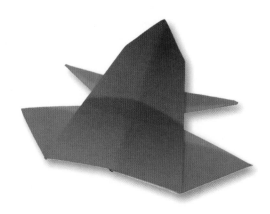

1 Begin by folding the collapsed triangle (page 182). Fold one edge to the center as shown. Notice that the top of the fold begins about one-fifth of the total length of the side, away from the top corner.

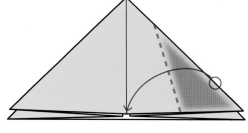

2 Fold your model in half vertically.

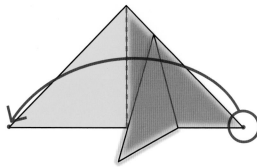

3 Fold the left edge of the top layer down, using the fold you made in Step 1 as a guide.

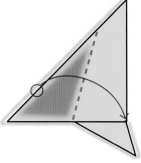

4 Fold the bottom corner of the top layer up and to the left as shown. This will create the frog's hind leg.

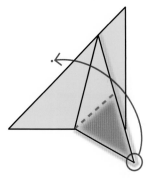

5 Your model should look like this. Book fold the top two layers to the right.

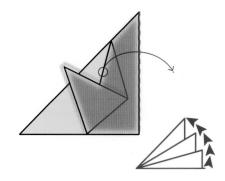

6 Fold the bottom corner up and to the right so it is identical to the one you folded in Step 4.

7 Fold the bottom left corner of the top layer to the top corner. Repeat on the other side of your model.

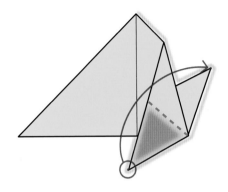

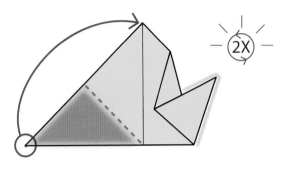

8 Your model should look like this. Fold the left corner of the top layer to the center as shown. Repeat on the other side of your model.

9 Your model should look like this. Inside reverse fold both folds you made in Step 8 to form the front legs of your frog.

10 Fold the flap you created in Step 9 down and to the left on both sides of your model.

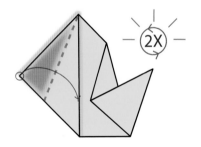

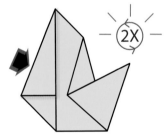

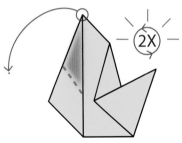

11 Fold the top layer of your model to the left as shown. Flip your model and do the same on the other side.

Your completed frog should look like this. Allow it to rest on its hind legs and the front legs will support the body at a very frog-like angle.

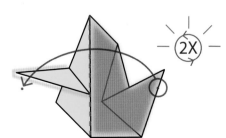

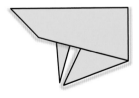

Folding the Rock Lobster

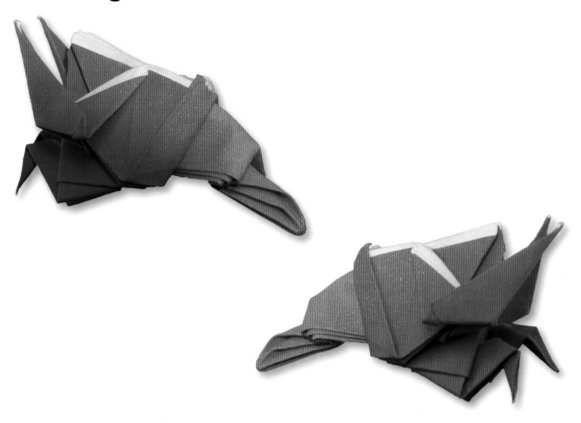

1 Begin by folding the collapsed triangle (page 182). Fold and then unfold the left and right corners of the top layer to the center.

2 Fold the bottom corners of the top layer down and to the center as shown. Flip your model and do the same on the other side. Do not perform Step 1 on the other side!

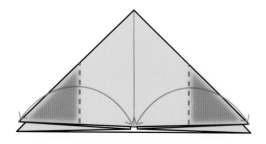

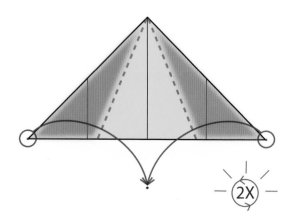

2X

3A One side of your model will look like this; the other will look the same but without the fold lines from Step 1. Inside reverse fold all four folds you made in Step 2. For additional help, look at the next diagram.

3B This diagram shows the direction of each fold after Step 3A is completed. Notice that the horizontal, vertical, and long diagonal folds are all valley folds. Notice that the shorter diagonal folds are all mountain folds.

If you're having difficulty completing Step 3, unfold your model and, with the colored side facing up, compare the folds to this diagram. Once you're sure each fold is in the proper direction, your square should collapse into a shape that looks just like the next diagram.

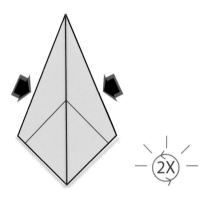

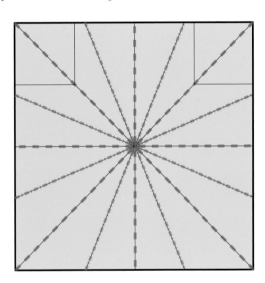

4 Inside reverse fold the folds you made in Step 1.

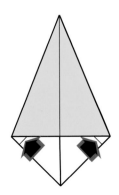

5 Fold the top flap (along with its associated subcomponents) up as shown.

(continued)

Folding the Rock Lobster continued

6 Fold the edges of the top layer to the center as shown.

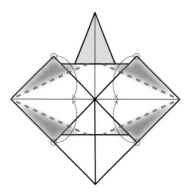

7 Close the fold you opened in Step 5.

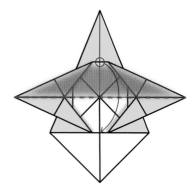

8 Your model should look like this. Flip it.

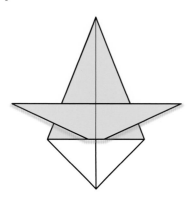

9 Fold the left and right corners of the top layer to the center as shown.

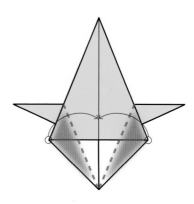

10 Inside reverse fold the folds you made in Step 9.

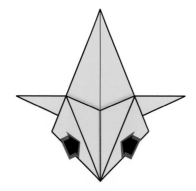

11 Fold and then unfold your model in half horizontally.

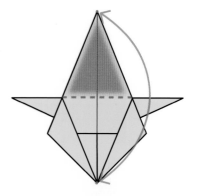

12 Lift the flap and…

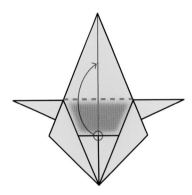

13 …crush fold the pockets that form.

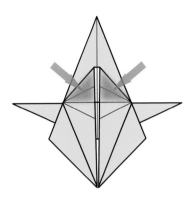

14 Book fold the corner indicated to reveal another flap.

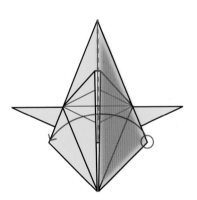

15 Fold and then unfold the left corner of the top layer to the center as shown.

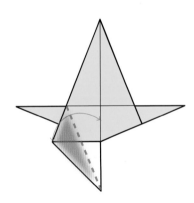

16 Open the top layer of paper as shown and…

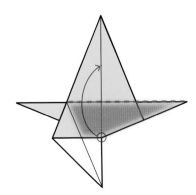

17 …crush fold the pocket that form.

(continued)

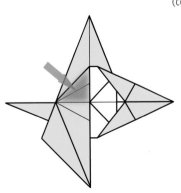

Folding the Rock Lobster continued

18 Close the flap you opened in Step 16.

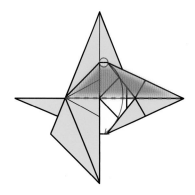

19 Repeat Steps 14 through 18 on the left side of your model. Make sure there are an even number of layers on both sides when you're finished. Your model should look like this.

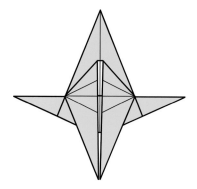

20 Inside reverse fold the highlighted area. See folding the lily (page 125) Steps 3A through 3C for more explicit instructions.

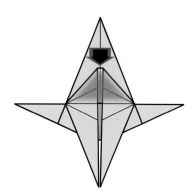

21 We now have a useful shape from which many animals can be made. You may want to experiment with this shape to develop models of your own design.

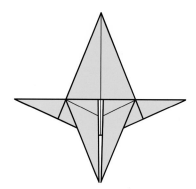

22 Fold and then unfold the lower right corner up and to the right using its inner edge and the paper's edge, as shown, for alignment.

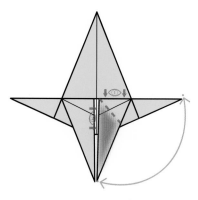

23 Fold and then unfold the lower right corner up and to the right using the fold you made in Step 22 and the paper's edge, as shown, for alignment.

24 Repeat Steps 22 and 23 on the lower left corner, and your model will look like this. T-fold the folds you made in Steps 22 and 23. If have trouble doing this, you may need to temporarily unfold the flap you closed in Step 18.

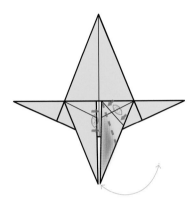

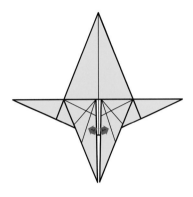

25 Fold the bottom tips along the vertical fold line as shown.

26 Outside reverse fold the folds you made in Step 25, and then flip your model.

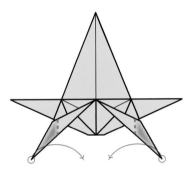

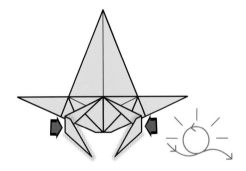

27 Fold the outermost corners of the top layer down and toward the center as shown.

28 Inside reverse fold the folds you made in Step 27.

(continued)

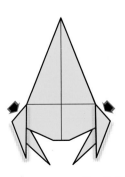

Folding the Rock Lobster continued

29 Fold the tips toward the outside as shown.

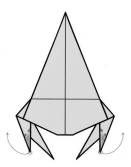

30 Inside reverse fold the folds you made in Step 29.

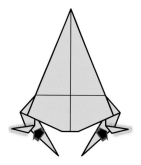

31 Your model should look like this. If you wish, you can fold two pairs of valley and mountain folds, as shown, to form a lobster-like tail; however, be careful so your model doesn't tear when you fold it in half in the next step.

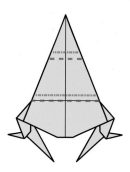

32 Fold all the layers of your model in half vertically.

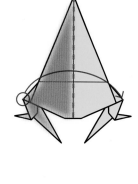

Your completed model should look like this.

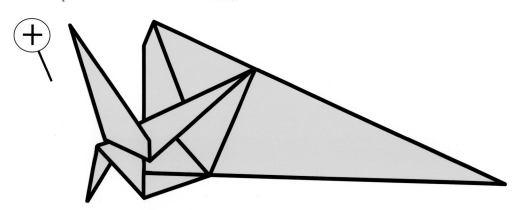

Folding the Hermit Crab

1 Begin by folding a collapsed triangle (page 182).

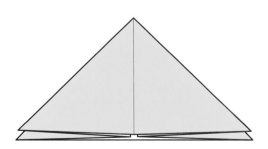

2 Fold the rock lobster (page 186) through Step 19, and then fold the bottom tips up and outward as shown.

(continued)

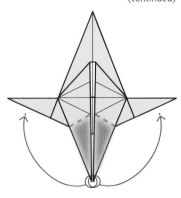

Folding the Hermit Crab continued

3 Inside reverse fold the folds you made in Step 2.

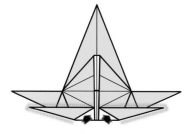

4 Fold the tips up as shown.

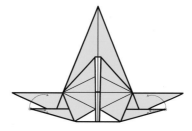

5 Outside reverse fold the folds you made in Step 4 and then flip your model.

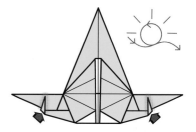

6 Fold the outermost tips up and toward the center.

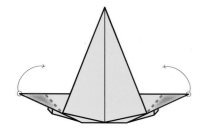

7 Outside reverse fold the folds you made in Step 6, and then flip it.

8 Complete your model by folding it in half vertically.

9 Your model should look like this. Pull the front legs out a little bit and crush fold the resulting flap just above the legs to create a free-standing model.

Your completed hermit crab should look like this.

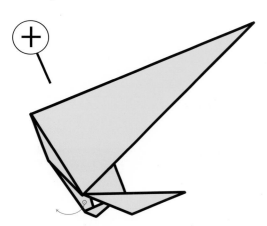

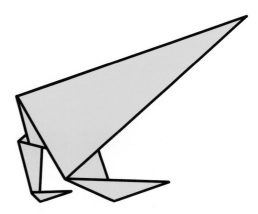

Folding the Three-Legged Gecko

Successful folding of this model requires that you pay close attention to book fold and flip symbols. In order to create a tail, we sacrifice a front leg. Because of this, the top layer of the finished model represents the tail, the two middle layers represent rear legs, and the bottom layer represents a forward stretching front leg.

1 Begin by folding a collapsed triangle (page 182). Fold the bottom corners of the top layer down and to the center as shown. Flip your model and do the same on the other side.

(continued)

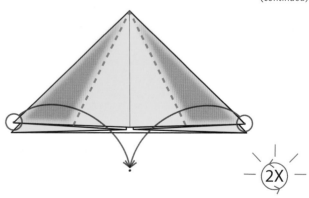

Folding the Three-Legged Gecko continued

2 Your model should look like this. Inside reverse fold the folds you made in Step 1.

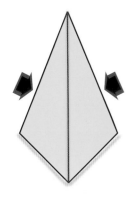

3 Your model should look like this. Fold the left and right corners of the top layer to the center as shown. Flip your model and repeat these folds on the other side.

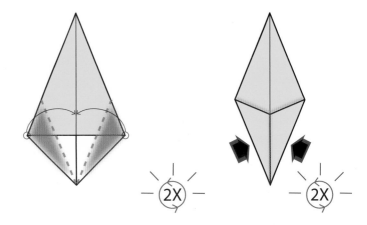

4 Inside reverse fold all four of the folds you made in Step 3.

5 Book fold (two layers on each side) your model and repeat Steps 3 and 4 on the other two sides. Your model should look like this. Fold and then unfold your model horizontally.

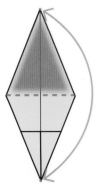

6 Fold the top layer of paper up as shown and then...

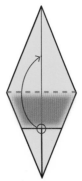

7 ...crush fold the little flaps that are created by the fold. Flip your model and repeat Steps 5 and 6 on the other side; then book fold and repeat on the other two sides.

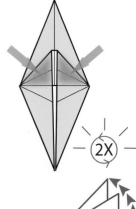

8 Book fold your model so that you have three points at the bottom of the left side and one point at the bottom of the right side. Flip your model to confirm that the other side looks the same (with the exception of three versus one tip) as this side. Fold the flap indicated in the diagram down on both sides of your model.

9 Your model should look like this (on both sides). Fold the right corner to the center, as shown, to narrow the tail. Flip your model and do the same on the other side.

10 Your model should look like this. Book fold precisely two layers from right to left.

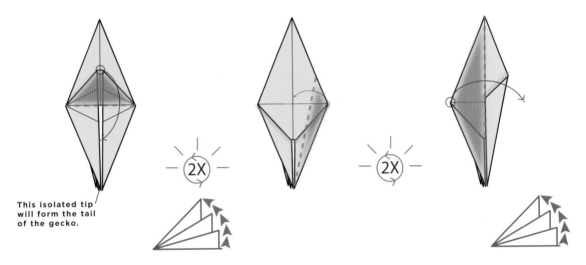

This isolated tip will form the tail of the gecko.

11 Fold the bottom right tip up and to the right to form one of the gecko's legs.

12 Your model should look like this. Inside reverse fold the fold you made in Step 11.

13 Book fold precisely two layers from right to left.
(continued)

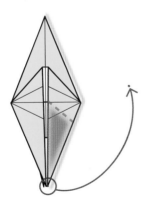

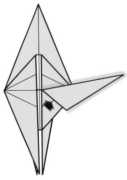

Folding the Three-Legged Gecko continued

14 Fold the bottom left tip up and to the left as shown.

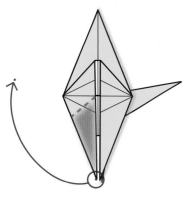

15 Inside reverse fold the fold you made in Step 14.

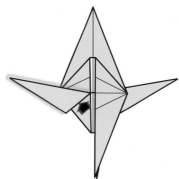

16 Book fold one layer from right to left.

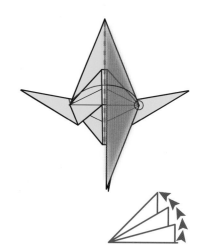

17 Your model should look like this. Fold the outer corners of the top layer to the center as shown.

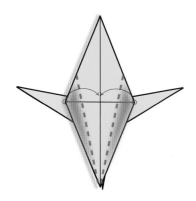

18 Close the flap you opened in Step 16.

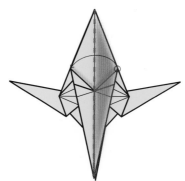

19 Fold the bottom left tip up and to the left.

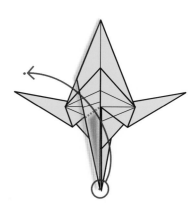

20 Inside reverse fold the fold you made in Step 19.

21 Your model should look like this. Book fold such that all three legs are on the left side of the model, including one layer of paper representing the tail on each side.

22 To form the head, fold and then unfold the top tip down to a point just behind where the back of the front leg intersects the body. You can also adjust the front leg by pulling it up and pinching at its base to secure it.

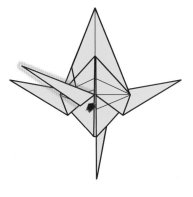

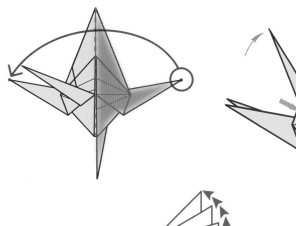

23 Fold and then unfold the tip down and to the left to a point midway on the front side of the front leg.

24 T-fold the folds you made in Steps 22 and 23. You don't need to secure this fold, and shouldn't try to. It is merely to add shape to the head of the model.

Your completed three-legged gecko should look like this.

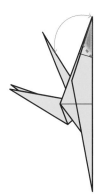

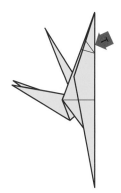

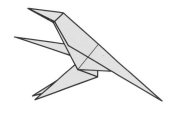

Folding the Sea Turtle

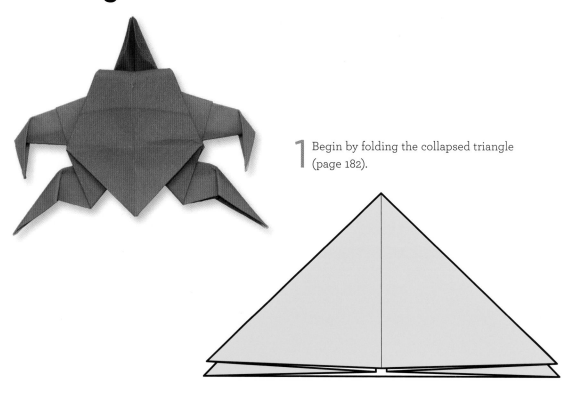

1 Begin by folding the collapsed triangle (page 182).

2 Fold the rock lobster (page 186) through Step 19. Fold the loose flap down, as shown, and then flip your model.

3 Fold the top two layers up.

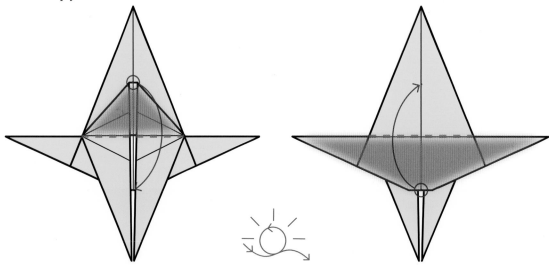

4 Your model should look like this. Fold the bottom tips outward as shown.

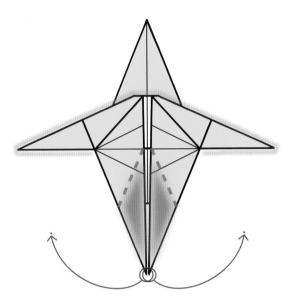

5 Inside reverse fold the folds you made in Step 4.

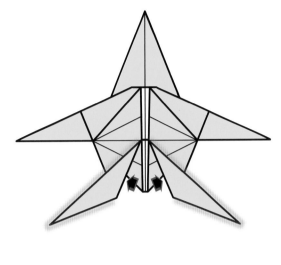

6 Fold and then unfold the bottom tips toward the extended center line of the model as shown.

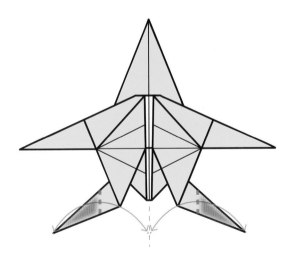

7 Fold and then unfold the tips down, as shown, using the fold you made in Step 6 to align them.

(continued)

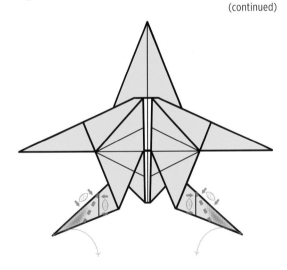

Folding the Sea Turtle *continued*

8 T-fold the folds you made in Steps 6 and 7.

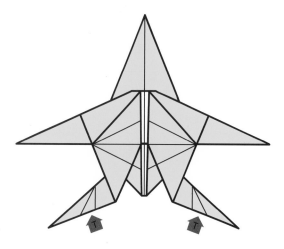

9 Fold the outside tips down and toward the center as shown.

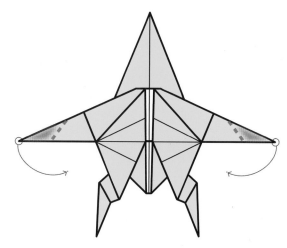

10 Outside reverse fold the folds you made in Step 9.

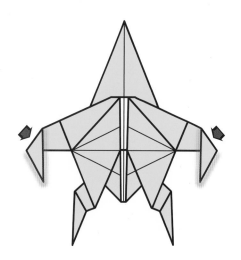

11 Fold the top corner down, just above the turtle's shoulders.

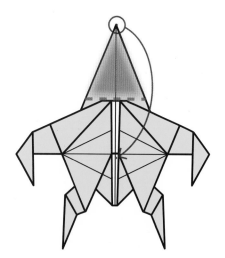

12
Fold the corner back up, leaving a gap as shown.

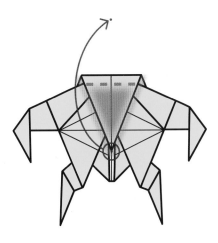

13
Your model should look like this. Flip it.

14
To shape the head, separate the top layer from the bottom three layers at the points shown in the diagram. Pinch the top (single) layer up and the bottom (three) layers down at the same time.

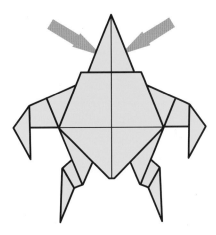

15
You can also give the flippers a little more shape by adjusting the T-folds (hind flippers) and outside reverse folds (front flippers). Your completed sea turtle should look like this.

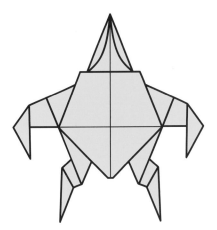

Folding the Brown Bear

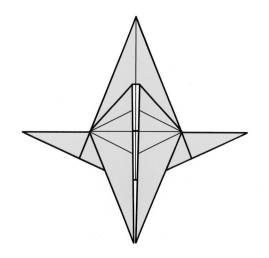

1 Begin by folding the collapsed triangle (page 182).

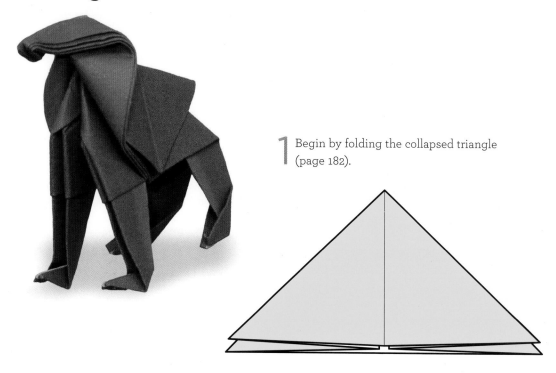

2 Fold the rock lobster (page 186) through Step 19.

3 Fold the sea turtle (page 200) through Step 5. Fold each of the outer tips up as shown. Notice that the fold lines for the upper tips are farther out than those for the lower ones. This is because we want smaller front paws.

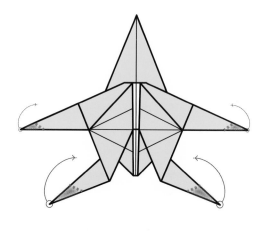

4 Inside reverse fold the front (upper) paws, and outside reverse fold the hind (lower) ones.

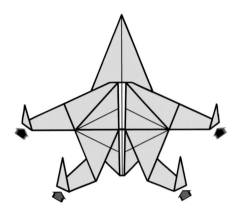

5 Optional: Tuck the tips of the paws into the reverse folds if you would like a more real-looking bear.

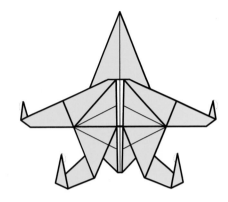

6 Fold your model in half vertically and reorient it so it matches Step 7.

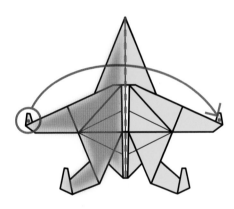

7 Fold the tip to the left as shown. This fold is just in front of the thickest part of the model.

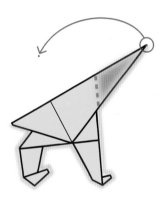

8 Outside reverse fold the fold you made in Step 7.

9 Fold the tip to the right, as shown, to form the head.

(continued)

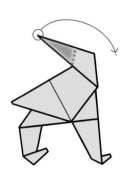

Folding the Brown Bear continued

10 Carefully (it is easy to tear the paper) outside reverse fold the fold you made in Step 9.

11 Fold a small amount of the tip inside to form the nose.

Your completed brown bear should look like this.

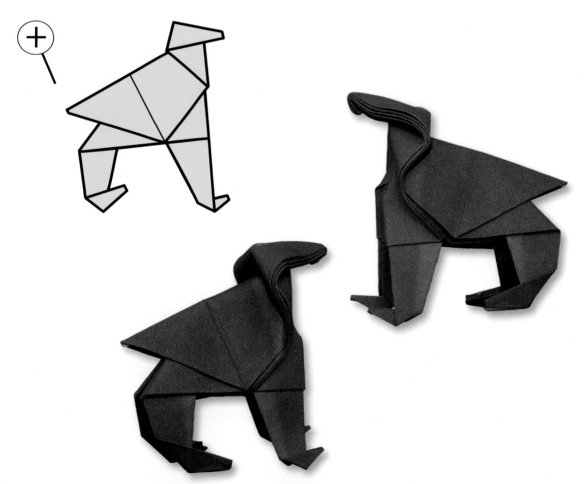

Folding the Hungry Fawn

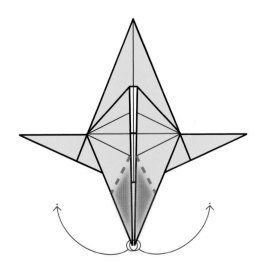

1 Begin by folding the collapsed triangle (page 182).

2 Fold the rock lobster (page 186) through Step 19. Fold the bottom tips up and out as shown.

3 Inside reverse fold the folds you made in Step 2.

(continued)

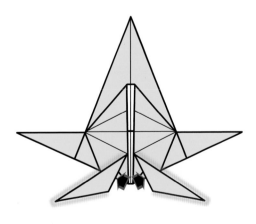

Folding the Hungry Fawn continued

4 Fold your model in half vertically, and reorient it so it matches Step 5.

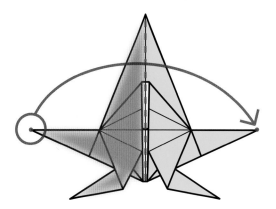

5 Fold and then unfold the tip down as shown.

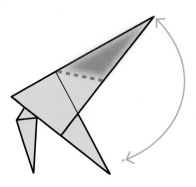

6 Fold and then unfold a second time, but a bit farther up the neck from the fold you made in Step 5.

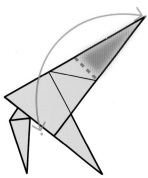

7 Inside reverse fold the fold you made in Step 5.

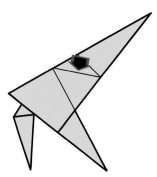

8 Inside reverse fold the fold you made in Step 6.

The fold line and edge are hidden beneath two layers.

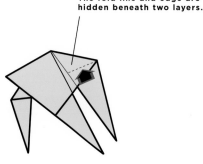

9 Your model should look like this. Fold and then unfold the top tip down.

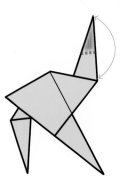

10 Fold and then unfold the top tip down and to the right.

11 T-fold the folds you made in Steps 9 and 10.

12 Fold the tip underneath to create a more deer-like nose.

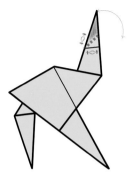

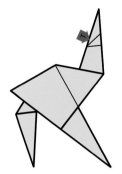

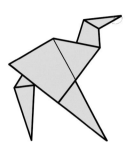

Your completed hungry fawn should look like this.

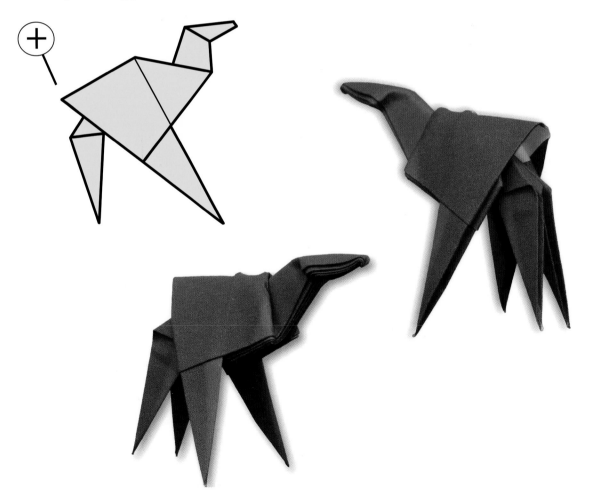

Folding the Fractal Geometric 2

TIP Fold all the layers of paper as shown in the steps that follow. Many of the folds in these diagrams will require reversing; therefore you should sharpen each fold as you perform it.

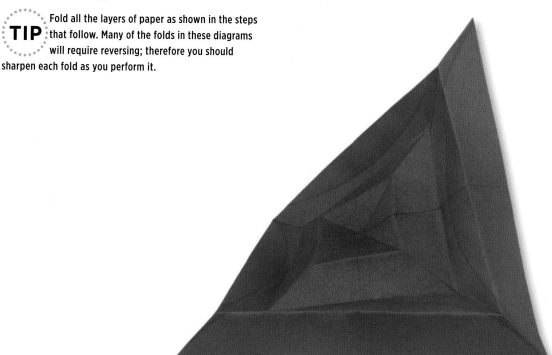

1 Fold the collapsed triangle (page 182) and reorient it so it matches the next diagram.

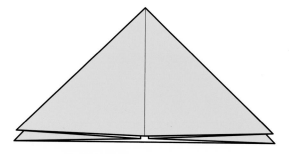

2 Fold and then unfold the bottom corner up to the top edge.

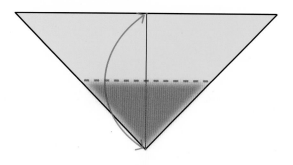

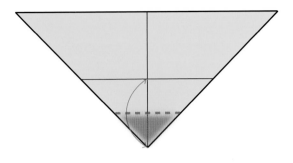

3 Fold and then unfold the bottom corner up to the fold you made in Step 2.

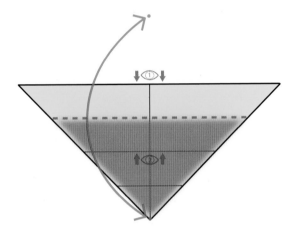

4 Fold and then unfold the bottom corner up using the fold you made in Step 2 and the upper edge of the collapsed triangle for alignment. Completely unfold your model.

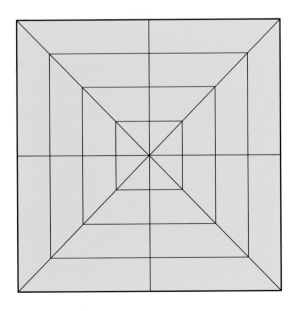

5 Your square should look like this.

(continued)

Folding the Fractal Geometric 2 continued

6 You will need to reverse almost half of the folds on your square. Here is a diagram that shows the proper direction of each fold. Notice that the longest horizontal and vertical folds won't be used.

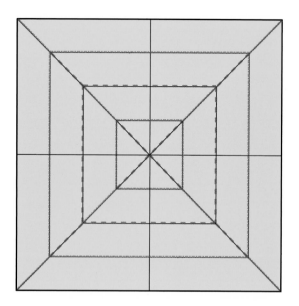

7 Work on the outermost folds first. Pinch a corner and reverse the folds. Allow the model to collapse into itself along the diagonals. Flip your model.

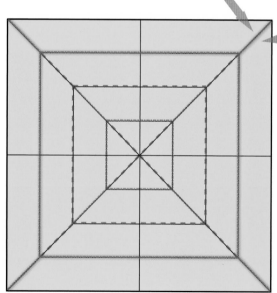

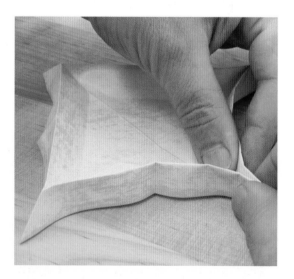

8 Now push and pinch until the folds reverse and collapse into the corners. Flip your model again.

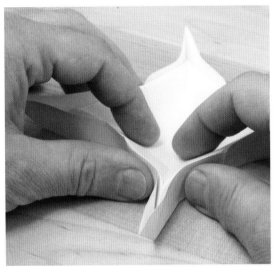

9 Push the smallest area into the shape and…

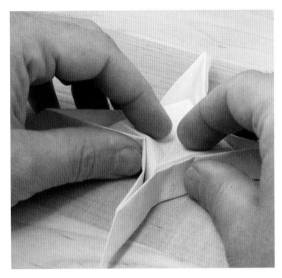

10 …collapse your model completely. It will form an X-shape.

11 Unfold your model and it will almost magically take this shape. This is the completed fractal geometric 2.

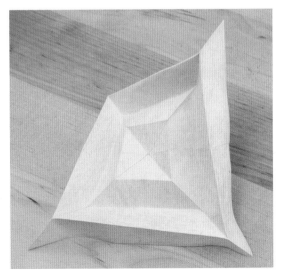

Other Things You Can Do

In Step 4, you can fold each area in half. This will create a much more complex model. Try using a larger piece of paper and see how many folds you can incorporate into your model in Step 4.

You can make a picture frame with this shape by folding longer folds only at the top of your model in Step 4. I added a crocus to my photo frame, made from one-fourth of a sheet of the yellow paper that comes with this book.

Folding the Human Being

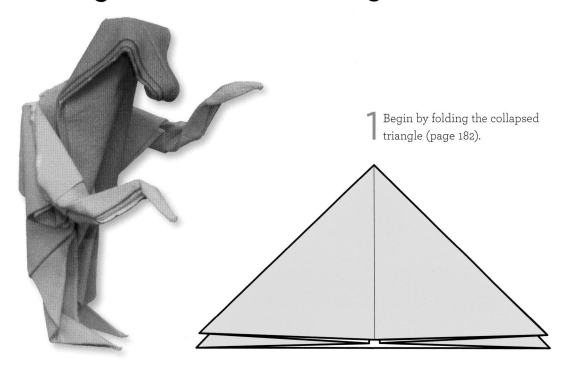

1 Begin by folding the collapsed triangle (page 182).

2 Fold the rock lobster (page 186) through Step 20. Fold the bottom tips up and out as shown.

3 Your model should look like this. Inside reverse fold the folds you made in Step 2.

(continued)

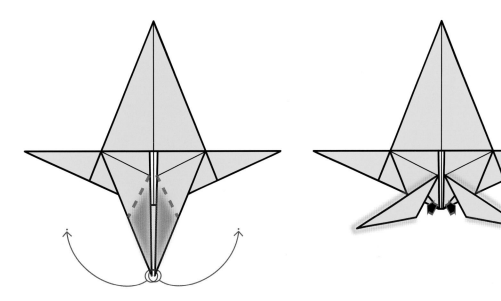

Folding the Human Being continued

4 Fold the top layers up as shown.

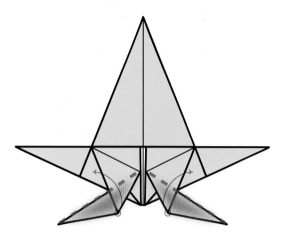

5 Narrow the bottom flaps by folding their outer edges to the center as shown.

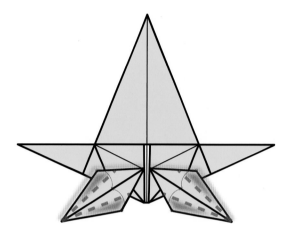

6 Close the bottom flaps.

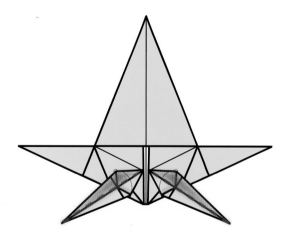

7 Fold both of the bottom areas up on the pre-existing fold.

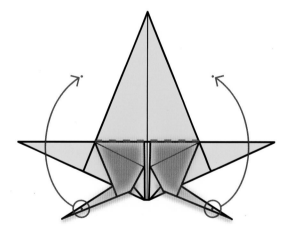

8 Align the edges as shown, and fold the outer corners down and toward the center.

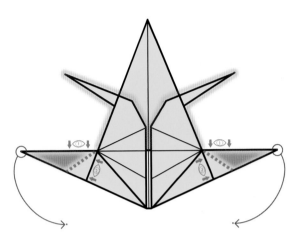

9 Inside reverse fold the folds you made in Step 8.

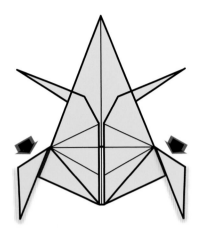

10 Your model should look like this. Fold the bottom outside corners up and toward the outside to form feet. Fold the top outside corners up and toward the center to form forearms (you may want to wait and fold the forearms at the very end of the project to create a specific pose).

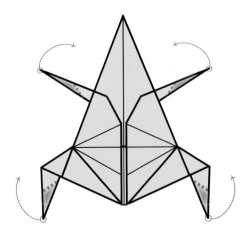

11 Inside reverse fold the feet and forearms.

(continued)

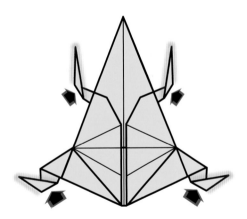

Folding the Human Being continued

12 Fold the upper tips toward the outside of the model, as shown, to form hands.

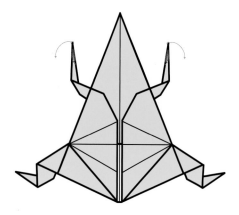

13 Inside reverse fold the folds you made in Step 12. Flip the model.

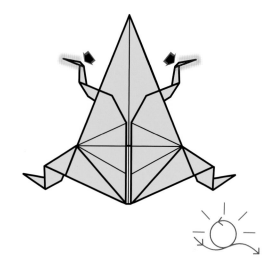

14 Fold your model in half vertically.

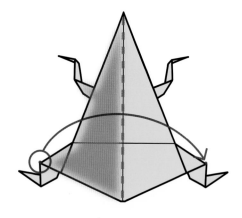

15 Fold the bottom corner up and to the right, as shown, to form the legs.

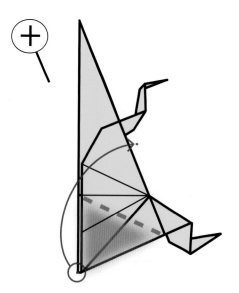

16 Inside reverse fold the fold you made in Step 15. After reversing, if the flap sticks out, fold it so it tucks inside neatly.

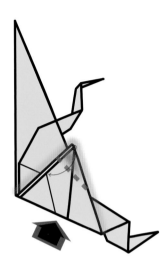

17 Fold the arm down at the existing fold to gain access to the layers of paper underneath. Repeat on the other side of your model.

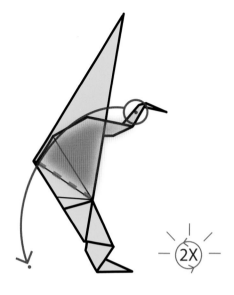

18 Fold the tip down and to the left as shown. You can feel where this fold belongs, as it is just ahead of the thickest layers of paper.

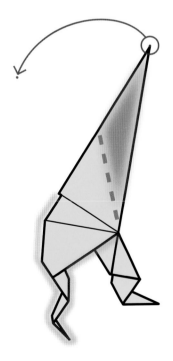

19 Outside reverse fold the fold you made in Step 18.

(continued)

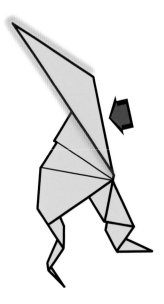

Folding the Human Being continued

20 Your model should look like this. Fold the top corner down and to the right to form the neck.

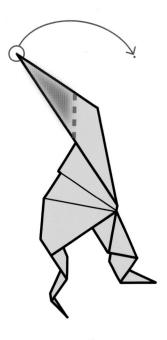

21 Outside reverse fold the fold you made in Step 20.

22 Fold and then unfold the top tip down and to the left.

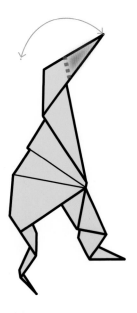

23 Fold and then unfold the tip down and to the left again as shown.

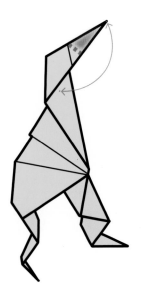

24 T-fold the folds you made in Steps 22 and 23.

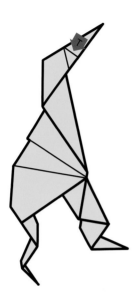

25 Your model should look similar to this. Lift the flaps that correspond to Step 23 away from the model.

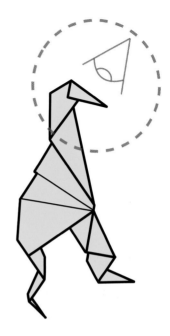

26 Pinch just behind the flaps while pushing the front surface to create a face on your model.

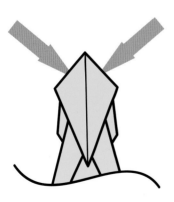

27 Tuck the bottom tip underneath.

(continued)

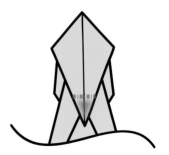

Folding the Human Being continued

28 Fold the arms back up, at the existing fold, on both sides.

29 Your completed human being should look similar to this. If desired, adjust the arms, and then adjust the feet and knees so your model will stand on its own. You can even fold the model's shoulders down (green dashed line) to change the overall look.

This is a complex model, that requires practice to be perfect.

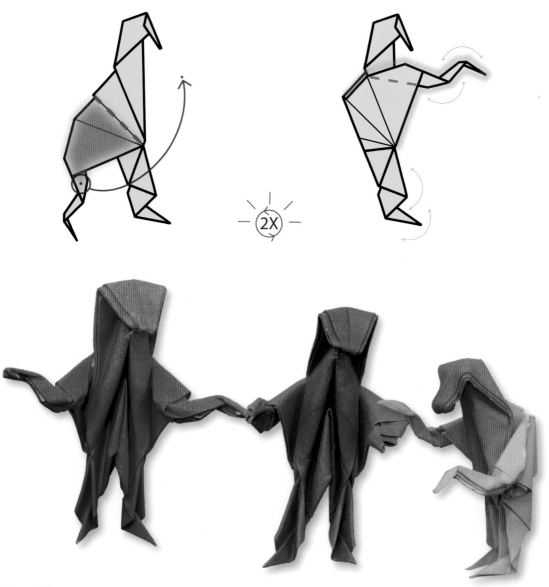

Symbol Index Bookmark

Glow and Afterglow p. 6

Fold p. 7

Flip p. 9

Fold and Then Unfold
p. 19

Alignment p. 21

Crush Fold p. 23

Pinch Fold p. 25

Mountain and Valley Folds
Basic p. 27
Detailed p. 131

Outside Reverse Fold
p. 29

Inside Reverse Fold
p. 33

Reverse Fold p. 37

Magnifying Glass p. 40

Fold on Both Sides
p. 43

Zoom Window p. 49

T-Fold p. 51

Zoom to a View p. 65

Collapse p. 83

Book Fold p. 87

Pull and Pinch p. 137

Glow and Afterglow p. 6

Flip p. 9

Fold and Then Unfold
p. 19

Alignment p. 21

Crush Fold p. 23

Pinch Fold p. 25

Mountain and Valley Folds
Basic p. 27
Detailed p. 131

Outside Reverse Fold
p. 29

Inside Reverse Fold
p. 33

Reverse Fold p. 37

Magnifying Glass p. 40

Fold on Both Sides
p. 43

T-Fold p. 51

Zoom Window p. 49

Zoom to a View p. 65

Collapse p. 83

Book Fold p. 87

Pull and Pinch p. 137